INDOOR GAMES THAT TEACH

Activities for Learning and Fun

by Robynne Eagan

illustrated by Gary Hoover

Teaching & Learning Company

1204 Buchanan St., P.O. Box 10
Carthage, IL 62321

This book belongs to

_____

Cover paper sculpture by Gary Hoover

Copyright © 1996, Teaching & Learning Company

ISBN No. 1-57310-068-4

Printing No. 987654321

Teaching & Learning Company
1204 Buchanan St., P.O. Box 10
Carthage, IL 62321

DEDICATION

To Vince, John, Gerry, Pat, Charlie, Ed and Rita for always having a game, a joke, a trick or a tale to lighten the spirit.

FOREWORD

Come on in and have some fun!

For hands-on, stimulating, educational fun and active learning, *Indoor Games That Teach* is just the thing. The games included in this resource have been specifically chosen to offer a stimulating variety of games to appeal to the abilities, learning skills and sense of fun of children in the K-4 grade levels. The resource includes a variety of cross-curricular games from the active to sedentary levels. The games provide opportunities to teach new skills and concepts, reinforce the development of skills and the learning of facts. Encourage socialization, cooperation and communciation and foster independent, creative thought.

ACKNOWLEDGEMENTS

I would like to recognize the many child specialists who have helped educators understand how children learn through play, especially David Elkind and my teachers Dr. Barb Park and Dr. Susan Langford. I would also like to thank all of those who passed games on to new generations, to those who recorded the games of the past, to those who first studied children's games and to those who first recognized the value of play in learning. A special thanks to Gerry Eagan for calling the square dance and for making all things fun. And finally, and most importantly, I would like to thank all of the children, educators, parents and game players who have shared their games, their ideas, their creativity and their fun with me over the years.

TABLE OF CONTENTS

Games in Education 7
Using Games in Education 8
Skills 9
Simple Ideas to Get You Started 10

Board Games

Make Your Own Gameboard 12
Gameboard 13
Floor Tile Gameboard 14
Mu Torere and Mu Torere Gameboard 15
Candy Checkers 17
Go Crackers! 18
Cooperative Scrabble™ 19
Nine Men's Morris 20

The Wonder and Fun of Words

Broken Telephone 21
Dictionary Guess/Made-Up Meanings 22
Rhyme Around the Circle 23
The Unfolding Story 24
The Pyramid of Words 25
Wonder Words 26
Grammar Pose/Kindergarten Pose 27
Secret in the Box 28
It Starts with 29
Listen and Record 30
Listening Bingo 31
Listening Bingo Card 32
Dice Fun 33

Roll a Story 34
Roll a Story Master Sheet 35
How Many Words Can We Make? 36
Tounge Twisters 36
Transpositions 37
Say It in Your Own Words 38
Make Your Own Crosswords 39
Repetitive Story 40
Magic Story Bag 41
The Mystery Character 42
Novel Characters/Name That Character 43
Musical Words 44
Sculpt with Words 45
Chalkboard Fun/Hangman 46
Sentence Match 47
Jokes and Graffiti 48
Identity Riddle Game 49
Hand Sings for Letters 50

Numbers and Logic and Mathematical Fun

Simple Number Games 51
Pot of Gold 52
Dice/Simple Dice 53
Scraps 54
Make Your Own Deck 55
Memory Match with Your Own Deck 56
Shuffle Those Cards .57
Snap 58
Add to 21 59
Shuffle Math 60
Number Guess 61
Marble Math 62
Minute Math Activities 63
Trading 64
Trading Colors 65
Dominoes 66

TLC10068 Copyright © Teaching & Learning Company, Carthage, IL 62321

Cooperative Dominoes 67
Tangram 68
The Tangram: An Ancient Chinese Puzzle 70
Math Toss 71
12 Up 72
Match the Measurement 73
Up the Wall 74
Guess How Many 75
Math Race 76
Indy 500 Racetrack .77
Chalkboard Number Maze 78

Problems and Mysteries Everywhere

What Did You See? .79
The Matching Game .80
I Love to Eat 82
What If? 83
Signs, Signs, Signs 84
Rubbings 85
Chalkboard Challenges 86
Square Designs 87
Can You Name That Can? 88
What Is It? 89
Details, Details, Details! 90
Chalkboard Mazes 91
Crack the Code 92
Baby Face 93
Odor Detective 94
Who's Undercover? .95
Line Up Race 96
Match 97
"Eye"dentify 98
Take a Close Look 99
Mapmakers 100
Paper Creations/Airplane 101
The Secret Letter 102
Fortune Teller 103
In Full View 104
Follow the Clapping Clues 105
Hide the Thimble 105
Pencil Games for Learning and Fun 106
Dots and Boxes 106
Tic-Tac-Toe 107

Action Games for Indoor Fun

This Is 108
Indoor Scavenger Hunts 109
The Alphabet Scavenger Hunt 110
Right Shoe, Left Shoe 111
Who Has the Beanbag?/Guess the Greeter 112
Time Out 113
The Iroquois Peach Stone Game 114
Charades 115
What Am I?/Laugh Master 117
Mirror Pantomime 118
Thumb Challenge 119
Dreidel Fun 120
Shadow Makers 121
Move to the Music and Stop 123
All in Together/Likes Attract 123
Square Dance 124
The Dance Call 126
Cooperative Musical Chairs 127
Touch Wood and Whistle 128
Indoor Hopscotch Math 129
Bounce and Count 130
Indoor Basketball 131
Takraw 132
Get It There Safely 133
Body Letters 134
Body Twist 135
Help Me Up!/Tied in Knots 136
Ready, Aim!/Beanbag Toss 137
Fan Ball 138
Indoor Golf 139
This Is a Ball 141
Indoor Races 142

Awards 143
Bibliography 144

Dear Teacher or Parent,

Observe a group of children at play and you will see learning at its best.

Play provides a medium for us to reach and teach young learners—games offer us a tool to do so. Games bring children together to participate and have fun while providing a natural learning environment where children have the opportunity to take risks, experience and understand the world around them.

Games provide a setting for children to have fun, use their ingenuity and creativity and master new skills and tasks. Games offer excitement, challenge and a natural platform for children to develop specific skills and acquire knowledge and to learn about personal success, fair play, cooperation and having fun.

From short transitional activities to long drawn out games of strategy and thought, *Indoor Games That Teach* is brimming with challenging games for indoor learning fun. The collection offers a variety of exciting activities that touch on all areas of the curriculum and appeal to children 5 to 10 years of age.

The hands-on learning fun will stimulate mental processes; challenge children to recall and develop new ideas; reinforce skills and facts; encourage emotional, social and creative development and lead young learners to make discoveries for themselves.

For a unique combination of laughter and learning, try a game!

Sincerely,

Robynne

Robynne Eagan

GAMES IN EDUCATION

Games allow children to:

- participate and explore new activities
- communicate in a variety of ways
- use their ingenuity
- develop healthy attitudes
- build bonds of friendship
- develop socially, emotionally, intellectually and physically

- develop skills of concentration, memory, creativity, problem solving and decision making
- learn about the meaning of numbers
- understand about order and sequence
- learn about the structure of language
- experience rhythm and rhyme

- focus and channel energy in stimulating activities
- develop awareness of body, emotions and abilities
- explore physical activities and enhance athletic abilities
- learn to manage healthy competition
- challenge themselves to do their best and appreciate their capabilities and limitations
- build independence, self-esteem and confidence in their abilities
- learn to play for the sake of playing

Benefits of Game Playing

Games make use of fun to facilitate learning. They provide a setting where learning and child development can occur in an unconstrained, natural manner.

Rules and Safety

Children between the ages of 5 to 10 are developing many social and emotional skills. In the excitement of a game, children may forget basic rules of conduct, safety concerns and social niceties. Gentle reminders and role modeling are necessary.

Ensure that the area is safe for all games being played.

With the children's input, establish rules and boundaries which are reasonable for your space. Consider things like noise level, taking turns, conflict resolution, acceptable game conduct, game etiquette, feelings involved with winning and losing and respect for others during a game. Make sure that the rules for safety and play are clear before the game commences.

USING GAMES IN EDUCATION

This at-a-glance information is provided for each game:

TITLE OF GAME

Grade Level • Number of Players • Curriculum Area • Activity Level • Duration • Cooperative

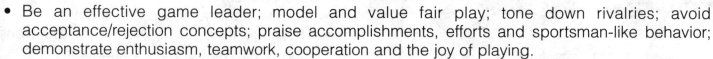

- Play the game for fun and the benefits will follow. The more fun a child has playing a game, the more he will seek to improve his skill at the game.
- Keep children interested by varying game activities. Be prepared to stop when the fun has gone out of an activity.
- Keep as many participants involved in the game, at any one time, as you can.
- Play a variety of structured and open-ended games–both offer fun and learning opportunities.
- Play a variety of cooperative and competitive games to provide kids with a valuable range of skills for life.
- Choose appropriate games to suit the physical coordination and cognitive abilities of the majority of participants. The game should be easily understood by the targeted age group.
- Be an effective game leader; model and value fair play; tone down rivalries; avoid acceptance/rejection concepts; praise accomplishments, efforts and sportsman-like behavior; demonstrate enthusiasm, teamwork, cooperation and the joy of playing.
- Demonstrate and expect respect for other players.

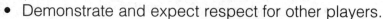

- Encourage children to play together–game interactions will help to build skills, confidence and friendships.
- Extend the fun and learning. Use any of the games in ways that suit your needs. Turn one game into another that has easier rules, changes the competitiveness or incorporates other skills. Let children change the games and invent games out of games. With a little creative thought, many games can be adapted to fit groups of other ages or sizes or to reflect the concerns and interests of a particular group of children.
- Approach games in various ways to promote targeted areas of development. A game can be a lesson or review in itself, a creative development activity, a simple transition or wake-up activity.

SKILLS

Game playing allows for experiences and the opportunity to acquire many skills. Play the game of active learning and watch skills and goals blossom along the way. Everyone is a winner!

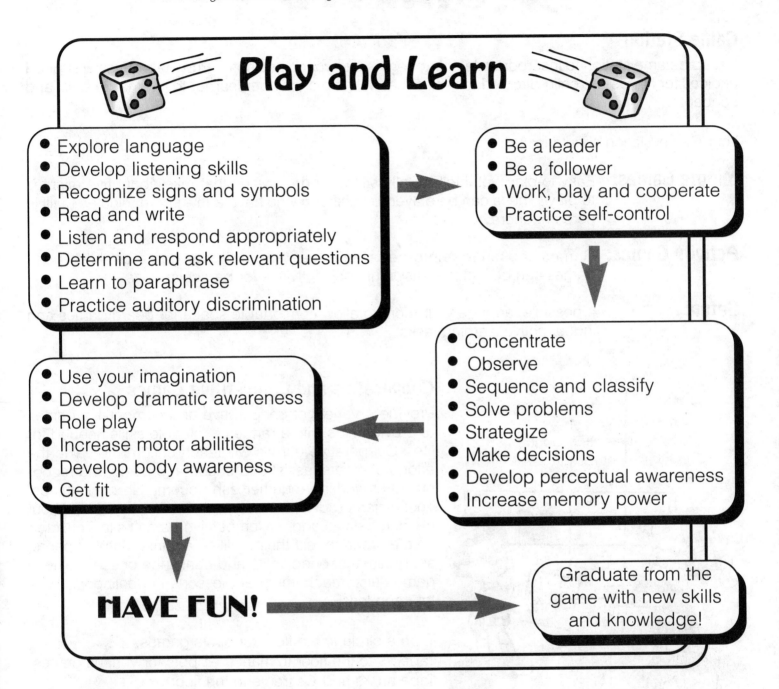

Play and Learn

- Explore language
- Develop listening skills
- Recognize signs and symbols
- Read and write
- Listen and respond appropriately
- Determine and ask relevant questions
- Learn to paraphrase
- Practice auditory discrimination

- Be a leader
- Be a follower
- Work, play and cooperate
- Practice self-control

- Concentrate
- Observe
- Sequence and classify
- Solve problems
- Strategize
- Make decisions
- Develop perceptual awareness
- Increase memory power

- Use your imagination
- Develop dramatic awareness
- Role play
- Increase motor abilities
- Develop body awareness
- Get fit

HAVE FUN!

Graduate from the game with new skills and knowledge!

Assessment

Games generally do not provide a medium for traditional methods of skill evaluation but do provide wonderful opportunities to record observational data and anecdotal comments. During game playing listen, observe and actively interact to determine communication abilities, reading and writing skills, understanding of numbers, problem-solving skills, fine and gross motor coordination and general creative abilities. Some games provide opportunities to record data on information recall the use of acquired skills.

SIMPLE IDEAS TO GET YOU STARTED

Game Station

Set up a game station to incorporate learning games into your classroom. Provide shelves with good choices for hands-on, child-directed activities that will help a younger learner to internalize skills and concepts.

Your Game Station should include:

Minute Games: Easy-to-play, yet intellectually stimulating activities that take about five minutes to play. These can be played by children who have a few spare minutes to fill in here and there.

Activity Games: Games chosen to reinforce or help teach a particular game or skill. These games can be included as "must do" activities for particular units.

Setup: If possible, arrange your room to allow comfortable space for board games and indoor active learning tasks.

Cooperative and Competitive Games

Provide a variety of cooperative and competitive games to provide kids with a range of valuable skills needed for life. Cooperative games will teach children to value the efforts of others, assist and encourage peers and recognize that working together can accomplish great things. These games demonstrate that fun can be had without the competitive edge. Competitive games allow children a safe arena to test their abilities against those of peers, set goals, test one's limits and challenge oneself. These games also teach important lessons in dealing with victory and loss.

Tape a circle to the floor for circle games.
Tape Xs to the floor to mark the spots for various games.
Tape an Xs and Os frame to the floor.
Tape a hopscotch grid to the floor for indoor fun.

Game Variations

There are many variations of particular games, even within the same school. This book offers a common version of favorite games.

BOARD GAMES

Go ahead, use a good board game as a teaching tool. Determine whether or not the game has educational value by asking yourself some simple questions. Does the particular game give children real life reasons to focus attention and concentrate? To read? To count? To problem solve? To learn facts? To socialize and cooperate? Does the game meet a need in a particular child? If you answer "yes" to one or more of these questions, then the game probably has a place in your classroom. Many games can be adapted to fit a particular unit or theme relevant to your group.

Don't forget the old favorites!

The tried and true board games are still popular for good reasons. They challenge, inspire, excite and educate. The following games will help to develop various skills and abilities:

Checkers	Chinese checkers	Chess
Monopoly™	Othello™	Battleship™
Mastermind™	Snakes and Ladders™	Clue Jr.™
Parcheesi™	Scrabble™	Trivial Pursuit™

Dear Parents:

Throughout the year, on occasion, we will be using learning games to help introduce new skills, reinforce concepts and further develop skills. Games provide the opportunity for education within the realm of childhood fun.

We are looking for the various items to stock our Learning Games Station and would appreciate donations of the following items:

Cards, Cards, Cards! We use playing cards for various math activities: sorting, counting, patterning, multiplication, division, problem solving and art activities.

Dice We will shake, rattle and roll our way through counting, adding, multiplication facts and storytelling.

Blank Cards These will be used as instruction, fact or trivia cards.

Game Pieces We can put your old gameboards and pieces to many good uses.

Thank you for your assistance,

_____
Your child's teacher

MAKE YOUR OWN GAMEBOARD

K-4 • Any Number • Understanding Rules/Language/Math • Hands-On • Medium

Materials

dice or pre-cut tag-
  board cards
tagboard or other
  sturdy material
pencils, markers,
  paints or
  crayons
playing pieces

*Packaging used
for our food, toys,
sports equipment
and other pur-
chased items
makes up one
third of the weight
of the garbage
each of us pro-
duces and it takes
up about half of
the space in our
landfill sites. Can
your game put
recyclable materi-
als to good use?*

How to Make It

1. Choose a theme for your gameboard. Are you learning about space? People of the world? Bears? Choose the type of path you want your game pieces to follow. Do you want to use numbers, letters, colors, characters or other means to mark the spaces on your board? You can use a repetition of three to six items related to your chosen topic.

2. Once you have made the decisions, design your gameboard on paper that is the same size you want your game to be.

3. Use copies, tracing or measurement, the sturdy board and marking materials to turn your rough draft into a finished gameboard.

4. Do you want to use dice or instruction cards to move pieces around? If using instruction cards, prepare these on the pre-cut cards. Design the cards to indicate the number of spaces a player may move forward or backward, to indicate the next space a player should proceed to or with questions that need to be answered before a move can be made.

5. Incorporate an art lesson into the design of the moving pieces. Consider plasticine, clay, foam sculpture, natural objects, found objects, coins or soft sculpture for your pieces.

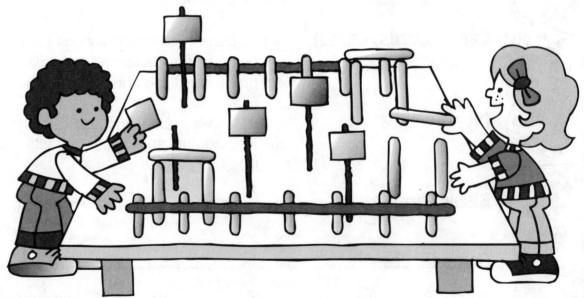

Try This

• Get creative! Try to make a 3-D gameboard using craft stick tunnels, pipe cleaner road signs, bread tie fences and so on.

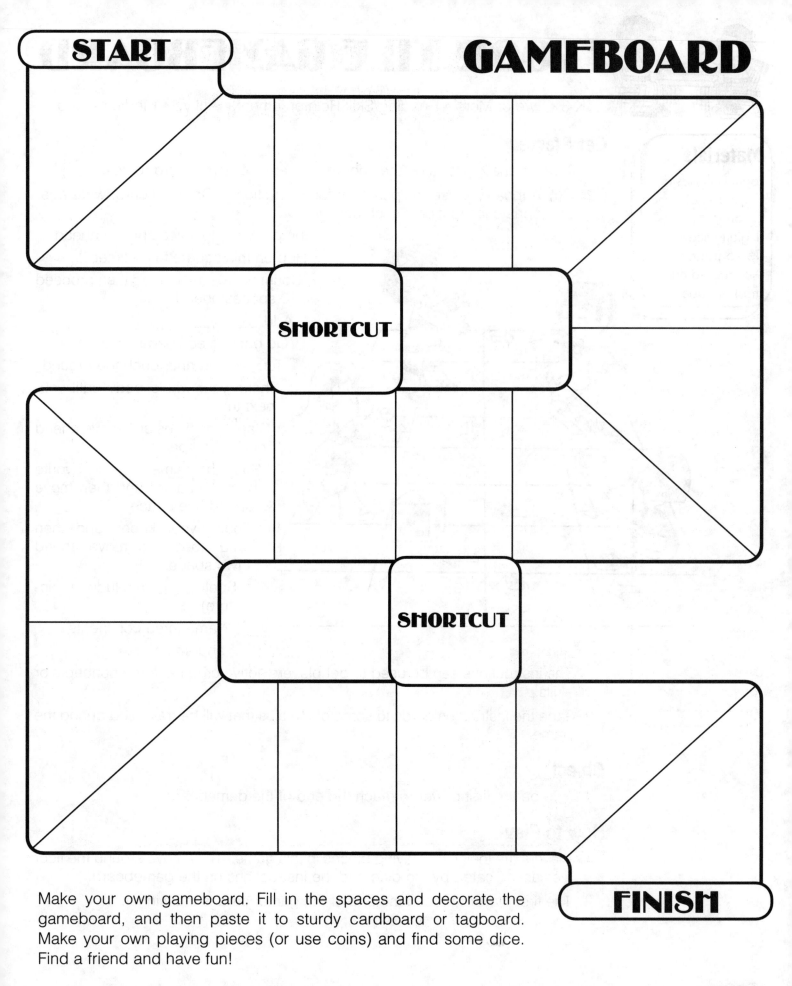

START

GAMEBOARD

SHORTCUT

SHORTCUT

Make your own gameboard. Fill in the spaces and decorate the gameboard, and then paste it to sturdy cardboard or tagboard. Make your own playing pieces (or use coins) and find some dice. Find a friend and have fun!

FINISH

FLOOR TILE GAMEBOARD

Transform your room into a board game!

K-3 • Two or More • Reading/Skill Reinforcement • Active • Medium-Long

Materials

room with tiles or squares of some sort
1 giant dice
15-25 paper or tagboard cards
masking tape

Get Started

1. Tape or chalk arrows on the floor to indicate the gameboard routes.

2. Cut tagboard or use recipe cards for instructions. On each card, write age-appropriate instructions, such as:

Jump on one foot two spaces ahead

Hop on this square three times

Count by 10s to 100 and then proceed 10 spaces ahead

Add ___ + ___

Go back three spaces

Turn around and touch the ground

Shake your whole body until your next turn

Clap three times and move ahead one extra space

Spell the name of your favorite book character and then move ahead one space

Touch your knees and then your toes and move ahead two spaces

Spell _____ (include a picture)

Name three continents

and so on . . .

The instructions can be used to get players active or to reinforce concepts or skills.

3. Tape the instruction cards to some of the tiles that will be traversed during the game.

Object

To be the first player to reach the end of the gameboard.

How to Play

1. Players are their own playing pieces in this game. They move around the floor tiles as indicated by the dice and the instructions on the gameboard.

2. The first player to reach the end of the gameboard is the winner.

MU TORERE

A New Zealand board game of strategy and fun

4 • Two or More • Multiculturalism • Strategy • Hands-On • Medium-Long

Get Started

Provide each player with a set of markers. Have players choose sides on the star. Players put their markers on adjacent points of the star on their side.

Materials

Mu Torere playing board (page 16) 2 sets of four markers (coins, dried beans, beads or buttons)

Object

To move pieces into a formation that makes it impossible for your opponent to move.

How to Play

1. The first player moves marker one or marker four into the circle in the middle of the star.

2. The second player moves her marker to the spot left vacant by the first player.

3. The first player moves another marker that leaves an empty spot for his marker.

4. Play continues in this manner until four moves have been made. Only one marker is allowed on a point or in the center at any one time. Players cannot jump over points but can move from one point to an adjacent point or into the middle circle.

5. Players move their markers onto the next points or into the middle as long as the spot is available.

6. After the first four moves, players use strategy to prevent the other player from being able to move her markers.

7. The player who sets up a situation where her opponent cannot move wins the game.

MU TORERE GAMEBOARD

Copy this Mu Torere gameboard and paste it to a sturdy surface ready for play.

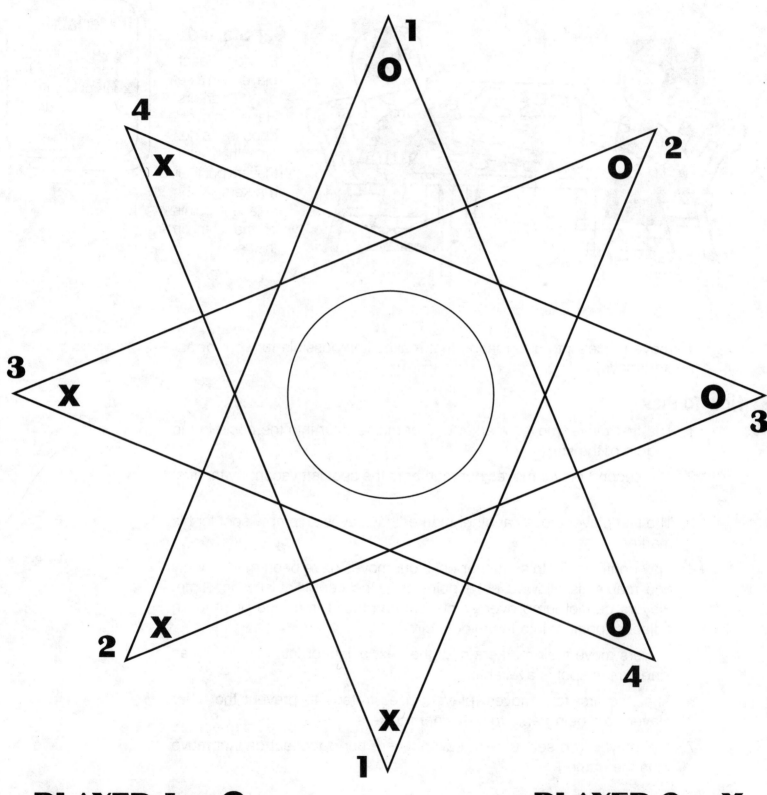

PLAYER 1 = O

PLAYER 2 = X

TLC10068 Copyright © Teaching & Learning Company, Carthage, IL 62321

CANDY CHECKERS

K-4 • Two or More • Strategy • Hands-On • Meduim

Get Started

Players sit on opposite sides of the gameboard.

Players set their candy pieces on the two rows of black squares closest to their end.

Object

To eat all of the other player's game pieces before she eats yours!

Materials

1 checkerboard
2 differing sets of 12 small candy pieces (gumdrops or Smarties™)

This modern version of checkers started in Europe in the twelfth century. A variety of unusual markers were used as playing pieces.

How to Play

1. The first player moves one of her pieces diagonally one black space, towards the opposing side.

2. The next player moves one of his pieces, one square at a time, and play continues in this fashion.

   A player may jump (and eat!) an opponent's candy piece when the opponent's piece is directly in front of the player's piece and there is an empty square directly beyond the opponent's piece. If there is another opponent's piece, followed by another empty square after the first formation, a player may jump two pieces in one turn.

3. When a player's piece reaches the opponent's end of the gameboard, that player may select any one of the opponent's pieces to take and eat.

4. The game is over when one player has eaten all of the opponent's pieces. At this point, as a show of goodwill, the winner shares her remaining pieces with the losing player.

17

GO CRACKERS!

Young children will learn to cope with the triumph of victory and the disappointment of defeat in this version of the ever-popular Snakes and Ladders™ game.

K-3 • Two to Four • Numeral Recognition/Game Patterns • Hands-On
Medium-Long

Materials

animal cracker cookies as playing pieces

small candies (Jelly Tots™ or Smarties™) placed at the tails of the snakes

Snakes and Ladders™ game

Get Started

Set up the gameboard. Place the candy pieces at the end of the snakes' tails.

Object

To be the first player to reach the end of the game.

How to Play

1. The first player rolls the dice and moves his piece the designated number of spaces. If his turn leaves him at the foot of a ladder, he "moves up in the game world" by climbing the ladder and getting nearer the end of the game. If his turn leaves him at the mouth of a snake, the player must move his piece down the snake and away from the end of the game. This little set back is compensated for by the little candy pieces placed at the tail of the snake. The candy can be eaten!

2. A player who rolls a six with the dice may take a second turn.

3. Play continues until one player reaches the end of the game and wins. All players may eat their animal crackers and divide any treats left on the gameboard.

Try This

• Make any game less challenging for little children who are learning to concentrate and deal with the emotions of victory and defeat. Allow players to move up the ladders *and* up the snakes.

18

COOPERATIVE SCRABBLE™

A cooperative version of the popular game of spelling and strategy.
Players of various ages and spelling abilities can play this one together.

1-4 • Two or More • Spelling • Hands-On • Medium • Cooperative

Materials

Scrabble™ game-board and letter tiles

Object

To make words that will lead to a high score for your group.

How to Play

1. Players choose letter tiles and play the game as in regular Scrabble™ but leave their tiles visible for all team members to see.

2. Players play their tiles in a way that will leave word possibilities for other team members and give *the team* the highest possible point score.

Variations

• Make up your own cooperative variations of other popular board games.

19

NINE MEN'S MORRIS

This very old English game is mentioned in William Shakespeare's play A Midsummer Night's Dream.

2-4 • Two or More • Strategy • Mild Activity • Medium

Materials

chalk
18 tokens (9 of one color or shape and 9 of another)

Get Started

1. On a small surface, draw a square about 1' (30 cm) on each side.
2. Inside the big square draw a smaller square. Inside the smaller square draw an even smaller square.
3. Draw four lines to connect the corners of the three squares.
4. Draw four lines to join the middle of each side of the three squares as shown.

Object

To remove as many of the other player's tokens as possible.

How to Play

1. Players take turns putting their tokens on the 24 intersection points of the gameboard.
2. Players attempt to place three tokens in a row along one straight line.
3. When all of the tokens have been placed, the players take turns moving one token at a time directly from one open point to another to place three in a row. When a player manages to get three tokens in a row, she may remove one of her opponent's tokens from the gameboard.
4. The game is over when a player has only two tokens left in play or is unable to make another move. In either case, the opposing player wins the game.

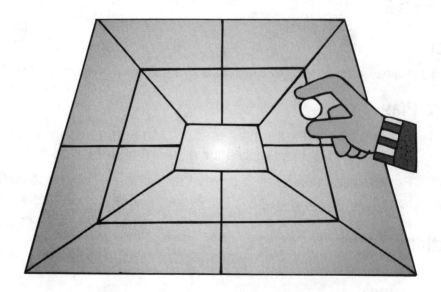

THE WONDER AND FUN OF WORDS

Words wonderful words! They are everywhere! From the moment children enter the world they are fascinated by words; their sounds, their meanings and their usage. Children from K-4 appreciate the sheer pleasure of words as they experiment, create and discover more about their usage.

Children revel in the simple joy of sounds, they shriek with delight at wacky word combinations, they are empowered by learning to make sense of words through play and communication and they learn to integrate into the world around them through the use of words.

This chapter will show you how to share the wonder of words and encourage the development of communication through oral language and the printed word.

BROKEN TELEPHONE

A simple old favorite that illustrates the importance of clear oral communication
1-4 • Group • Oral Communication • Sedentary • Short • Cooperative

Get Started

Players sit on the floor in circle formation. Choose one player to make up the original message.

Materials
none

Object

To pass a whispered message around the circle.

How to Play

1. The Messenger whispers the message into the ear of the player to her right or left.

2. This player whispers the message into the ear of the player on his other side . . . and so on.

3. The last player to receive the message must repeat what she heard to the group.

4. The player who initiated the whispering reveals the original message.

DICTIONARY GUESS

This game is great for building vocabulary.

2-4 • Group • Verbal • Sedentary • Short • Cooperative

Materials

1 dictionary

Get Started

Choose one player to be "Keeper of the Dictionary."

Object

To reveal the meaning of the selected word.

How to Play

1. Keeper of the Dictionary opens the dictionary to any page, closes her eyes and points to a word. Keeper then opens her eyes and pronounces the word.

2. If one player in the group knows the meaning of that word, the Keeper must select another word.

3. Play continues until the Keeper chooses a word that the entire group does not know the meaning of. When such a word is found, Keeper may sit down and choose another for her job.

MADE-UP MEANINGS

3-4 • Group • Vocabulary Building • Sedentary • Medium

Materials

1 dictionary

Get Started

Divide the group into two teams and select a "Keeper of the Dictionary."

Object

To determine the real meaning of a selected word.

How to Play

1. Keeper selects a word from the dictionary, reads it to the group and writes it on the board. He then writes the meaning on a piece of paper.

2. Players make up a meaning for the word and write it on a piece of paper.

3. Keeper collects the phony definitions and the real definition in a box and then reads them to the group.

4. Players attempt to guess which definition is the real definition. Players who recognize the true meaning of a word are awarded two points for their team. Players receive one point anytime their definition is mistaken for the real one.

5. The team with the most points at the end of the game wins the match.

RHYME AROUND THE CIRCLE

Just for the rhyme of it!

1-4 • Group • Sedentary • Short • Cooperative

Materials

Get Started

Have players sit on the floor in circle formation. Select one player to choose the first rhyming word.

Object

For all players in the circle to contribute a word that rhymes with the original word.

Boat!

How to Play

1. The Rhymer clearly announces the rhyming word.

2. The player on his right states a word that rhymes with the word.

3. The next player in the circle offers another word . . . and so on.

4. If a player has difficulty, he may turn to players on the left and right of him for help. Those players may turn to players on their other sides and so on until a word is found.

5. The circle of players can take pride when all players come up with a rhyming word and the group is able to rhyme around the circle.

Variation

RHYMING SHOWDOWN

In this fast-paced version of Rhyme Around the Circle, each player has only 10 seconds to come up with a rhyming word. Players who cannot come up with a word on their own are eliminated from the game. By the end of this game two poets will engage in a rhyming competition showdown that will delight the audience.

THE UNFOLDING STORY

2-4 • Groups of 10 • Storytelling/Writing/Creativity • Sedentary • Medium

Materials

10 sheets of paper
pencil for each player
Format List

Get Started

Seat players at a writing desk, and provide each with a pencil and one piece of paper. Display a Format List as shown below.

Format List

1. _____, _____ One or more adjectives.

2. _____ The name of a person or pet.

3. _____ One verb.

4. _____, _____ One or more adverbs.

5. _____ Pronoun GAVE.

6. _____ The name of a person or pet.

7. A/AN _____ Adjective.

8. _____ A noun.

9. EVERYONE _____ verb.

10. _____ adverb.

Object

For players to help complete a story with no knowledge of any other elements of the story.

How to Play

1. Instruct players to begin, at which time each player writes one or two words as dictated by the Format List.

2. After one minute, have each player fold his paper to hide what has been written and all papers are passed to the right or left.

3. Players now write one or two words on the blank section of paper as dictated by Format List.

4. Players once again fold and pass the paper on the time signal.

5. The game continues until each player has written a word or two for the 10 different requests.

6. When each player has finished writing number 10, the papers are passed once more.

7. In turn, players read aloud the paper they are holding.

THE PYRAMID OF WORDS

2-4 • One or More • Problem Solving/Language Skills • Sedentary • Medium

Fill one letter in each box to complete a word on each line. Continue until all levels of the pyramid are filled. Can you complete the pyramid in five minutes?

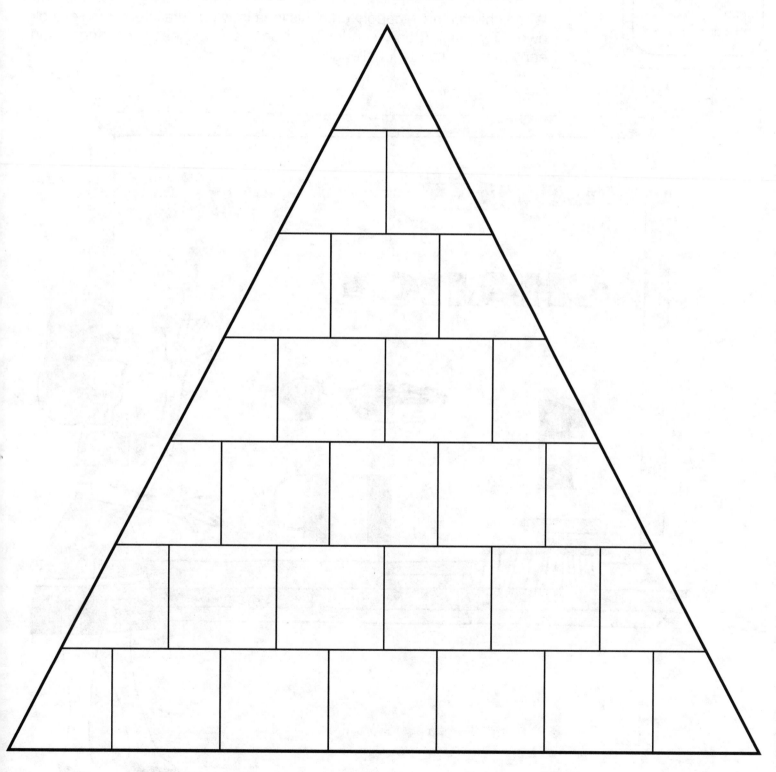

WONDER WORDS

2-4 • Group • Problem Solving/Language Skills • Sedentary • Short

Write these "wonder words" on the chalkboard. Can children discover the meaning of each one?

When children have caught onto this idea they can make up some of their own. Try placing one wonder word on the board each morning for an early morning mental challenge.

GRAMMAR POSE

1-4 • Three or More • Drama/Grammar • Active • Medium • Cooperative

Materials

slips of paper
spotlight (optional)

Get Started

Ask students to write either nouns, verbs, adjectives or adverbs on slips of paper. Put the slips in a box.

How to Play

1. A selected player takes a slip from the box, reads it and hands it to the teacher or game leader.

2. The player strikes a pose to reveal the word on the paper.

3. Players in the group try to guess the word being demonstrated.

4. The player who guesses the correct word chooses a slip and strikes the next pose.

KINDERGARTEN POSE

K-1 • Three or More • Drama • Active • Medium • Cooperative

Materials

drawings or pictures of animals

Get Started

Choose a player to go first. Put pictures of animals in a box.

How to Play

1. One player takes a picture from the box, looks at it and hands it to the leader.

2. The player then strikes a pose to represent the picture.

3. Players in the group attempt to guess the animal being represented by the pose.

4. The player who guesses correctly picks a picture and prepares the next pose and so on.

Try This

• Teachers or leaders can help break the ice by taking the first pose.

SECRET IN THE BOX

2-4 • Three or More • Oral Communication/Problem Solving • Sedentary
Short or Long

Materials

paper and pencil
small box with a
lid

Get Started

Decorate a box with question marks. Choose one player to be "Secret Maker." Select a category that the secret must fall into–a peer, a hero or heroine, a story character, an animal, a rock or mineral, a place, a means of travel or other relevant item to your studies. Secret Maker chooses a word that must fall into the predetermined category. He writes the word on the paper and puts the paper in the box to be revealed when the item is guessed.

Object

Secret Maker tries to choose an object that will not be guessed in 20 questions. Guessers attempt to guess the word before the 20 questions have been used up.

How to Play

1. Secret Maker reveals the category her item falls under.
2. Players raise their hands and fire questions that require only a "yes" or "no" answer.
3. Guessers may ask no more than 20 questions.
4. If the item is not guessed after 20 questions have been asked, Secret Maker must reveal the item and may take another turn.
5. If a player guesses the item, then he will become Secret Maker for the next round of the game.

Strategy

- Ask questions wisely. Ask questions that address a broad spectrum before trying to narrow the guessing to specific items. For example, "Is it alive?" "Is it larger than an elephant?" "Does it have fur?"

IT STARTS WITH . . .

K-3 • Any Number Can Play • Language • Sedentary • Medium

Materials

1 piece of paper and pencil for each child

Object

To fill quadrants of the paper with lists of words beginning with particular letters of the alphabet.

How to Play

1. Provide each child with paper and pencil.

2. Have children fold their paper into quarters.

3. In each quarter children should write headings given by the teacher or leader. Consider the following: countries, food, famous people, places, book titles, sports, activities, occupations and so on.

4. When children are prepared, the leader or teacher calls out one letter of the alphabet.

5. Children fill each section of their papers with as many words as they can think of that start with that letter and meet the criterion for the particular section. Young players may draw pictures of these things, rather than write them down.

LISTEN AND RECORD

K-1 • Group • Listening/Auditory Discrimination • Hands-On • Medium

Materials

tape recorder or partition

sounds: hammer, whistle, telephone, bell, running water, wind, raindrops, bird songs, instruments, singing voice, radio, clock alarm and so on

pencil and paper for each child

Get Started

Prepare a tape with various sounds. Leave about two seconds of silence at either end of the sound.

or

Set up a partition to shield an assistant from the group. Behind the partition, set up a table with various sound makers behind the partition. Provide each child with pencil and paper.

Object

To correctly identify the sounds heard.

How to Play

1. Children are provided with paper and pencil.

2. When players are ready, turn the tape on or have the sound maker begin to make sounds behind the partition.

3. Players record the word or picture to describe the sounds they hear. Players number guesses to correspond to the sequence of the sounds. Instruct players to leave blanks and move on to the next sound if necessary.

30

LISTENING BINGO

K-1 • Group • Listening/Auditory Discrimination • Hands-On • Medium

Get Started

Prepare a tape with various sounds. Leave about two seconds of silence at either end of the sound. Prepare bingo cards by cutting pictures from magazines and other sources of the various sounds. Have children glue these pictures (only one of each sound on each card) into the spaces on sturdy bingo cards that have been photocopied onto stiff paper or recycled cards in which you cover the numbers

Materials

tape recorder or partition
sounds: hands clapping, hammer, whistle, telephone, bell, running water, wind, raindrops, bird songs, instruments, singing voice, radio, clock alarm, etc.
magazine pictures
sturdy cards
bingo chips

Object

To correctly identify the sounds heard.

How to Play

1. Provide each player with a bingo card and a handful of bingo chips.

2. Turn the tape on to play the collection of sounds.

3. When a player hears a sound that is shown on her card, she covers the square with a bingo chip.

4. The first player to get a complete row of markers may call out "bingo" and wins this round of the game.

Variations

• Players must completely fill a card before being allowed to call out "bingo."

• Put children in charge of preparing the tape and cards.

LISTENING BINGO CARD

Copy this page and paste in the pictures for your bingo game.

DICE FUN

A set of dice and this game model can provide any number of classroom theme-related games.

K-4 • Two to Five Players • Versatile Game Possibilities • Hands-On

Short or Long

Get Started

Prepare a Dice Task Board that gives instructions for each face of the die or paste the task instructions to the faces of a large die. See task examples below.

Object

To roll the die and complete all of the required tasks.

DRESS UP LIKE A FIREFIGHTER

If you roll a . . .

1. Put on the firefighter's boots.
2. Put on the firefighter's hat.
3. Put on the firefighter's coat.
4. Take the firefighter's hose.
5. Wear the firefighter's badge.
6. Take any item you need.

or

DRAW A PERSON

If you roll a . . .

1. Draw the head with a face.
2. Draw the neck and shoulders.
3. Draw the body.
4. Draw arms and hands.
5. Draw legs.
6. Draw the feet.

How to Play

1. The first player rolls the dice and completes the instruction given for the face of the die.

2. The second player rolls and completes the specified action and so on.

3. Play continues in this manner until one player completes all of the tasks.

Materials

dice
instruction board
(stiff cardboard
and markers)
gameboard or
items for particular game

ROLL A STORY

This game is just the thing for young authors with writer's block!

2-4 • One or More • Writing/Creativity • Hands-On • Long

Materials

2 dice
pen or pencil and
    paper for each
    player

Get Started

Copy the Roll a Story Master Sheet or make one of your own following the same format.

How to Play

1. Each player must roll five times–once for each category.

2. When the dice have been thrown, a player must match the sum of his throw with the corresponding number on the Master Sheet and record the information cited for that roll.

3. Play continues in this manner until each player has rolled and recorded for each part of the story.

4. When the player has all of the required information, he puts pencil to paper or fingers to keyboard and writes his tale.

34

ROLL A STORY MASTER SHEET

Who are you?

2–a gold digger
3–an astronaut
4–a famous hockey player
5–an ostrich farmer
6–a baby
7–a mountain climber
8–a parent
9–a rodeo rider
10–a detective
11–a teacher
12–a treasure hunter

Why are you worried?

2–you can't find your glasses
3–it is getting very, very cold
4–no one recognizes you
5–someone is looking for you
6–you don't know your way
7–you lost all of your money
8–your vehicle is having technical
   problems
9–your best friend moved
10–your dog is missing
11–you lost your memory
12–you are the only one who knows how
   to save the world

What are you doing?

2–looking for your lost pet
3–learning to play the banjo
4–learning how to surf
5–you have just found a flying saucer
6–climbing a mountain
7–you have just found a secret map
8–dancing on stage
9–hiding from a crazy old farmer
10–watching a baseball game
11–going to a university
12–jumping from an airplane

How are you going to solve your problems?

2–by asking Mom for help
3–with ingenuity and creativity
4–by running away
5–by looking up Old Smoky Joe
6–by contacting the leader
7–with help from friends
8–by talking to a fortune teller
9–by getting advice from a book
10–by going to the police
11–with researching
12–by using your magic powers

When is the story taking place?

2–in present day
3–in the year 2000
4–in the future at least 1000 years
5–in the year 1642
6–in the 1800s
7–in the winter
8–in the summer
9–in the middle of the night
10–in the heat of mid-noon
11–in the olden days
12–at harvest time

Where are you?

2–on a boat in the ocean
3–living in the forest
4–in your bed
5–on the highway
6–in a barn
7–in the Arctic
8–in a secret tree house
9–falling through the sky
10–sitting at a computer keyboard
11–in the school yard
12–in a dark cave

HOW MANY WORDS CAN WE MAKE?

This simple transition activity builds vocabulary, enhances spelling skills and develops creative thinking.

1-4 • Group • Language Skills • Sedentary • Cooperative

Get Started

Write one word on the chalkboard. Use a big word such as *transportation*, *technology*, *intelligent*, *alphabet*, *gymnasium* or *mathematics*.

Object

To derive as many words as possible from the letters used in the word on the board.

How to Play

1. Draw children's attention to the word on the chalkboard.

2. Ask children to make as many words as possible from the letters in that word. Children may first work independently, making their own list, or the groups can work together volunteering words and recording them on the board.

3. Go for 100 words if you can!

TONGUE TWISTERS

There are many favorites to twist your tongue.

K-4 • Any Number • Oral Language/Communication/Recall • Sedentary • Short

Think of three things.

She sells seashells by the seashore.

Grim ghosts grin.

Betty Botter bought a bit of bitter butter.

Double bubble gum doubles bubbles.

If Peter Piper picked a peck of pickled peppers,
Where's the peck of pickled peppers Peter Piper picked?

A filly frolicked in the flowers.

36

TRANSPOSITIONS

Scrambled letter fun to develop skills of spelling and creative analysis!

4 • Any Number • Word • Sedentary • Short

Object

To decipher the scrambled words to make one word.

How to Play

1. Write various word groups on the board. See examples below.

2. Have players attempt to decipher the scrambled words to make one word.

3. Players who decipher all of the words may come to the board and add some transpositions of their own for others to solve. Players will have fun working from the word to the transpositions or vice versa.

purse cash	cool cheat	nurture fir	a mild bear
purchases	*chocolate*	*furniture*	*admirable*

SAY IT IN YOUR OWN WORDS

2-4 • Group • Language • Active • Medium-Long

Get Started

Divide the group into two equal teams. Teams line up on opposite sides of the playing area and face one another.

Stamp your feet.

Object

To repeat what another has said in your own words.

How to Play

1. The first player on Team 1 proposes an action to the first player on the opposing team. For example, "Stamp your feet."

2. The first player from the opposing team must do the action and then repeat it back to the original player in her own words, i.e. "Lift up one sole and put it on the floor loudly and then do it with the other sole." She may not use any of the words given in the original instructions.

3. The original player must then do the action as described.

4. If both players perform the tasks appropriately, both teams get a point. If the player from Team 2 was not able to rephrase the action, then only Team 1 receives a point.

5. When all players on Team 1 have proposed actions, play starts again with Team 2 providing the actions.

38

MAKE YOUR OWN CROSSWORDS

This exercise will call on children's knowledge of spelling, word meanings and problem solving.

2-4 • Two or More • Spelling/Problem Solving • Hands-On • Short-Medium

Materials

chalkboard
graph paper
pencil
ruler

Get Started

Prepare young learners for this activity by doing some ready-made crossword puzzles. When children have mastered an understanding of these word puzzles, you are ready to begin. Provide children with the materials listed.

Object

To create a crossword puzzle for peers to complete.

How to Play

1. Have children design their own crossword puzzles. Start with simple five-word puzzles and increase the puzzle size as children master the required skills.

2. Photocopy each crossword puzzle at least once and have students exchange puzzles and complete one created by another child.

Variations

• Have children create crossword puzzles based on a relevant topic, theme or on their personal word list.

• Allow students to transcribe their crossword puzzles to the chalkboard. Others may work on the puzzle throughout the day, when their assignments are completed.

REPETITIVE STORY

A fun game that incorporates sequencing, memory and association.

K-4 • Two or More • Language/Memory • Sedentary • Short • Cooperative

Materials

Get Started

Players get in circle formation and choose a story starter such as:

"When I go camping, I take . . . "

"When I go to Grandma's house, I take . . . "

"Out on the street I pass . . . "

or any other other starter that suits a theme you are studying.

Object

To repeat what another has said.

How to Play

1. The first player repeats the story starter and adds one item to the list.

2. The player to the right or left of the first player repeats the story starter, the previously mentioned item on the list and then adds an item of her own.

3. Play continues in this manner with each player repeating and adding a new item to the list.

40

MAGIC STORY BAG

K-4 • Group • Storytelling • Sedentary • Medium • Cooperative

Get Started

Purchase or make your own interesting story bag. Cut 20 pieces of tagboard into squares, circles or idea clouds. Have children cut interesting pictures from magazines, photos and newspapers. Glue the pictures to the tagboard shapes. *Do not tell the children what these pictures will be used for.* Put the picture cards into the Magic Story Bag.

Object

To contribute a line to the story based on a picture taken from the story bag.

How to Play

1. Have players sit in circle formation.
2. Hand the bag to the first player. He reaches in and takes out a picture.
3. He starts to tell the story based on the picture card he picked.
4. The bag is passed to the next player in the circle. He removes a picture and continues the story incorporating this picture and so on until the last person in the circle finishes the tale.

Variation
ADD-A-LINE STORIES

Players sit in circle formation and tell a story as above without the story prompting pictures from the Magic Story Bag.

Strategies

- Situate children with strong storytelling abilities at the start and end of the circle to ensure a strong start and a tidy conclusion to the story.

- Record the story for later reference for children and parents.

There was a cat . . .

THE MYSTERY CHARACTER

2-4 • Groups of Four • Drawing/Creativity/Following Instructions
Hands-On • Medium • Cooperative

Materials

pencil for each player
large sheets of paper

Get Started

Divide children into groups of four. Fold papers into quarters and write a small number in the corner of each section. Seat groups at a large table or on a hard floor and provide a pencil and one sheet of paper for each child. Ensure that the top folded section is visible for drawing on.

Object

To contribute to a drawing of a character without viewing the other parts.

How to Play

1. Have each player draw a head in section 1. The neck should extend just beyond the paper fold, into section 2.

2. When the timer sounds, players fold the paper to expose a blank section and pass the paper to their right. Each player will be passed a re-folded paper ready for them to draw on. Players may not look at what others have drawn. On the signal, players draw the neck to waist portion of the character in section 2.

3. When the timer sounds, players extend the waist lines and draw to the knees in section 3, fold the paper and pass it on.

4. The process continues until section 3 is drawn and ankles to feet are drawn in section 4.

5. At the end of the exercise the papers are unfolded and participants take great delight in seeing the usually humorous characters they helped to create.

Variation

• You may choose to add more detail and make more folds by adding separate sections for hair, shoulders, legs and feet.

42

NOVEL CHARACTERS

1-4 • Group • Reading/Communication/Information Recall • Mild Activity • Medium

Get Started

Read a story or study a novel. Write the names of characters from the story on the tagboard cards.

How to Play

1. Tape one card to the back of each student.

2. Students circulate around the classroom asking questions that will help them discover their "novel identity." Questions asked may require only a "yes" or "no" answer.

3. When a player has determined his correct identity, the tag is moved from his back to his chest. He then continues to answer questions until all players have discovered their identities and the game is over.

Materials

tagboard cards
marker
masking tape

NAME THAT CHARACTER

1-4 • Group • Communication/Information Recall • Mild Activity • Cooperative

Materials

slips of paper
container

Get Started

Study a particular novel as a group. Write the names of characters from the book on slips of paper and place them in a container.

How to Play

1. One player selects a slip of paper from the container. She must then describe the characters to the other players without revealing specific names, places or events mentioned in the story.

2. The group attempts to identify the character presented. The player who correctly guesses the identity chooses a character from the container for another round of the game.

Variation

• The above games can be played using explorers, historical figures, Presidents, musicians, farm animals, wildlife, insects or other entities being studied.

MUSICAL WORDS

2-4 • Groups • Musical • Mild Action • Long

Materials

chalkboard and chalk

pencil and paper for each child

timing device

Get Started

Divide the group into two teams. Choose a word that is found in popular songs. Some good word choices include *love, home, baby, Christmas, cry, birds, rain* and so on.

Object

To sing more songs than the opposing team.

How to Play

1. The leader or teacher writes one word on the chalkboard and sets a timer for one to two minutes.

2. Team members think of and write as many songs as they can that contain the word on the chalkboard.

3. When the timer sounds, teams stop writing and prepare for song competition and the fun begins.

4. The first team sings a portion of a song that contains the word.

5. The second team sings a portion of another song containing the word.

6. The teams sing back and forth until one team

can no longer come up with a tune and forfeits the match.

SCULPT WITH WORDS

K-4 • Two or More • Movement/Language/Vocabulary • Active • Medium

Get Started

Divide the group into pairs.

Materials

Object

To use words to sculpt a partner into a particular shape. To be shaped by a partner's words.

How to Play

1. One partner takes the role of sculptor and the other becomes the clay.

2. The sculptor shapes the clay with words, for example, "Bend at the wrist," "Stretch your arm towards the door," "Tilt your head toward the floor."

3. When the masterpiece is completed, the sculptor shows her work, to the rest of the class or group.

4. The partners reverse roles and the artistic process begins again.

CHALKBOARD FUN

The chalkboard provides a visual medium that focuses children's attention, brings lessons to life and allows for group lessons and shared experiences. This simple resource can be put to good use in many creative ways. Use the board to provide visuals when possible and to highlight lessons. Keep lots of colorful chalk on hand, allow children to use the board and don't forget the magnetic possibilities of this teaching tool.

HANGMAN

This old favorite is still appreciated for its challenge and educational value.

1-4 • Two or More • Game Skills/Spelling/Analysis • Hands-On • Short

Get Started

Choose one player to select the first word and lead the game. The game leader draws the gallows as shown in Figure 1.

Object

To fill in the blanks and guess the word before your man is hung.

How to Play

1. The game leader chooses a word, draws lines to represent the letters in the word and reveals a category the word falls under. Usual categories are a person, a place, an animal, a book title, a movie and so on. Teachers might ask that words be connected to a particular theme.

2. The guesser or guessers take turns selecting possible letters in the word. If a guess is correct, the leader writes the letter on the appropriate line or lines. If a guess is incorrect, the leader writes the incorrect letter above the gallows and draws one body part in the gallows.

   IT hopes to complete the entire body before the guessers guess the word. The guessers hope to complete the word before the body is hung.

3. A player who completes the word may be IT for the next round. If the body is completed, as shownin Figure 2, before the word is guessed, then the man is considered "hung" and the game is over.

4. IT then chooses another word and the game begins again. If the word is guessed, the guesser is IT for the next round and chooses a new word and prepares the gallows.

Strategies

- As all words contain vowels, it is wise to start your guessing with the vowels and proceed with some of the more commonly used consonants.

Variation

- If you find the "hanging" concept a little too grim, you can change the game to "Diver." Ice cold water is drawn at the bottom of the diagram and the body is drawn part by part, to dive into the ice cold water.

Figure 1   Figure 2

 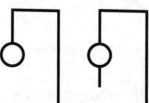 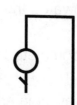   

SENTENCE MATCH

3-4 • Group • Grammar/Language Skills Reinforcement • Sedentary
Medium-Long

Get Started

Prepare the following columns on the chalkboard:

Determiner   Adjective   Noun   Verb   Adverb

Scramble four sentences into one word list that runs beneath the columns. There should be 20 words in all. For example, scramble: *The funny dog ran quickly.* The child who puts these words together in their correct columns will gain three points for his group. Choose one person to be the Recorder and write words in the columns as the game is played. Divide the group into two teams.

How to Play

1. In turn, have players from opposing teams choose a word from the word list to put in a particular column. When a word is correctly assigned to a column, the Recorder crosses it off the word list and puts it in the column. When a player assigns a word to the correct column, she gains one point for her team and may attempt to guess an entire sentence. If the player guesses an entire sentence, she gains three points for her team.

2. Play continues in this format until all words have been placed in their correct columns and the four sentences are reconstructed.

3. The team with the greatest number of points when all of the words have been placed is the winner.

JOKES AND GRAFFITI

Nonsense and Jokes and Riddles!

1-4 • One or More • Language/Communication • Sedentary • Short

Materials
chalkboard and chalk

Object

Leader: To encourage reading, writing and creative thought.

Players: To read and solve the joke or riddle.

How to Play

1. In the morning or after a recess, write a riddle or joke on the chalkboard.

2. Players are to sit in their seats and solve the joke and riddle. The player who knows the answer writes it on the board. If this player is correct, he may add a new joke of his or her own.

Try some of these jokes to tickle young funny bones.

The greater it is the less it is seen.
What is it?
The dark

I picked a basketful and started to cry.
What did I pick?
Onions

When is a dog not a dog?
When it's a puppy

What do you get when you cross a cat and a lemon?
A sourpuss

Why did the fly fly?
Because the spider spied her
Spell mousetrap in three letters.
C-A-T

What runs on and on and never stops?
A creek

Which dog has the best time?
A watchdog

Why are horses such bad dancers?
Because they have two left feet

Variation

• One chalkboard can be designated the graffiti board. Throughout the day, children who have completed their assignments may use their reading, writing and artistic abilities to decorate the board, leave riddles, puzzles or clever sayings for others to enjoy.

48

IDENTITY RIDDLE GAME

2-4 • Group • Oral Language/Creativity • Mild Activity • Short

Get Started

Choose one child to leave the room. Have players form a circle and choose one student to be the Cool Dude.

Object

IT: To discover the identity of the Cool Dude through the riddles.

Players: To make up a riddle about the Cool Dude that is not too revealing.

How to Play

1. The player sent out of the room is called to return as players think up riddles about the Cool Dude.

2. Players form a circle, including the Cool Dude, and the child returns to the room.

3. In turn, around the circle, each child shares a riddle that offers a clue to the secret identity. Players may not use names in their riddles.

4. A child may pass but must try to offer a riddle on the next turn, or the next or the next. No player can use the name of the secret someone.

5. When the identity of the Cool Dude is guessed, another player is chosen to leave the room.

HAND SIGNS FOR LETTERS

A challenging new slant on spelling and reading for most of us

2-4 • Two or More • Substitution/Spelling/Reading/Concentration • Hands-On
Medium • Cooperative

Get Started

Provide each participant with the hand spelling chart for study and practice. Have the group break up into pairs. Have children prepare containers with one-, two-, three-, four- and five-letter words written on slips of paper. Provide one set of containers for every four children participating.

How to Play

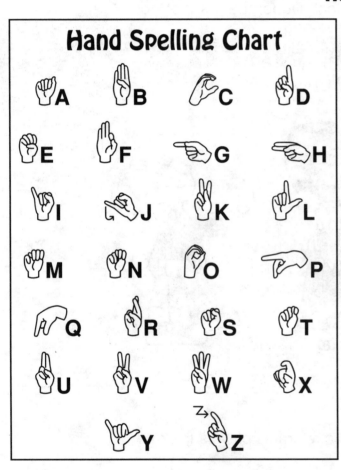

Hand Spelling Chart

1. When children are familiar with the hand alphabet, have them find a partner.

2. Partners should begin by hand signing the alphabet together.

3. When all partner groups are ready, they are grouped with another pair. One member of the first team takes a word from the "one-letter word cup" and hand spells it for her partner, no more than twice. Her partner translates the hand spelling and pronounces the word. If this team has correctly communicated the word, they receive a point or points corresponding to the number of letters in the spelled word, and play passes to the next team. On their next turn, the first team will attempt to communicate a two-letter word and, if successful, will proceed to a three-letter word on their next turn and so on to the five-letter words. If the team was unsuccessful, they do not receive a point and will attempt to communicate the particular lettered word on their next turn.

4. The second team selects and communicates a one-letter word in the same manner and so on.

5. The first team to collect 15 points wins the match.

Variation

• For noncompetitive play, partners will enjoy signing the hand sign alphabet by taking turns spelling and translating words.

NUMBERS AND LOGIC AND MATHEMATICAL FUN

Almost every game challenges players to use some form of mathematical ability. Fast-paced active games encourage players to reason, strategize, estimate and make quick decisions. Many games call on players to recognize patterns, estimate, interpret and make predictions. Games encourage young learners to sharpen their skills of estimation, measurement, problem analysis, number recognition, addition and subtraction and problem solving. The games in this chapter are aimed at developing logic and mathematical abilities. They are intellectually challenging, reinforce a variety of math concepts and are amusing and educational at the same time.

SIMPLE NUMBER GAMES

There are many simple games that will captivate young children who have discovered the wonderful world of numbers and counting. Use your imagination to make numbers relevant and fun.

K-2 • Group • Verbal/Concept • Sedentary • Short • Cooperative

Materials
a child's everyday environment

Get Started

Take a closer look at your surroundings and find ways to use it to assist with counting and number recognition.

Object

To count things in the environment. To recognize numerals in the everyday environment.

How to Play

Pose a simple number finding or number recognition activity to the group and watch what happens! Try the following suggestions or come up with some of your own:

- Take a number hike around the school and look for numbers, look for pairs or look for a specific number.

- See how many number ___'s you can find in two minutes.

- Where can you find the numbers 1 to 12 in your classroom? (Check the time!)

- Hike to the grocery store. Why are numbers important here?

- How many eyes/buttons/shoes/boys/girls . . . are there in this classroom?

POT OF GOLD

Looking for the perfect game for St. Patrick's Day?

K-2 • Two • Coin Recognition/Counting/Graphing • Hands-On • Medium

Materials

10 "gold coins"
   (shiny pennies)
10 "silver coins"
   (dimes)
flat playing surface
recording page
felt

Get Started

Make your "pot of gold" by cutting a pot out of black felt. Provide each player with 10 pennies, 10 dimes and a page to record their results.

Object

To gain experience recording, comparing and understanding money.

How to Play

1. The first player drops her handful of coins from above the "pot of gold." The coins that fall on the pot are recorded on her personal recording page.

2. The second player drops coins and records the results and so on until each player fills their recording page.

3. Each player adds up how many dimes and how many pennies landed in the pot altogether. Who had more pennies? Who had more dimes? Players may then figure out the value of the money they had drop in the pot. Who has more now? Did the player who had the most coins land in the pot also have the highest value of coins?

Variations

• Have some fun with the results. Have children add the results of their throws to a pictograph. Use real coins for effect. Did more pennies or dimes land in the pot?

• Make up some word problems based on this game.

52

DICE

Dice are wonderful tools for introducing children to counting and adding. Each roll of the dice offers a new counting or adding challenge. With experience rolling the dice children will come to instantly recognize the dot formations as representations of particular numbers and in no time they will recall that certain combinations equal particular sums.

Materials

shaker cup
die
20 counter pieces (Smarties™, coins, buttons or pebbles)

SIMPLE DICE

K-1 • Two • Number Recognition/Addition • Mild Activity • Medium

How to Play

1. Player 1 rolls the dice and identifies the number rolled. If she correctly identifies the number, she is awarded a counter and may roll again. This player continues until she makes an incorrect guess and play passes to her opponent.

2. Player 2 rolls, counts and collects counters in the same manner until all of the counters have been distributed.

3. Players take inventory of their counters.

4. The player who possesses the most counters wins the game.

Variation

TWO-DICE PLAY

Participants play as above but use two dice instead of one and reveal the sum of the dice.

SCRAPS

A simplified, modified version of an ancient dice game that is quite appropriate for children who are learning to count up those dots and become familiar with number concepts.

2-4 • Two • Number Recognition/Counting/Game Rules • Hands-On • Medium

Get Started

Familiarize players with the terms and rules as follows. These are easily picked up after a few rounds of the game. Determine who will roll first.

Rules

A roll of seven or 11 takes the pot.

A roll of snake eyes or boxcars loses the player his turn.

A roll of any number but 2, 12, 7 or 11 is called a *point*, which must be matched for a player to win the pot. A player who rolls a *point* rolls the dice until she rolls a match and wins the pot or rolls the unlucky seven or 11 and her turn is *scrapped*–her turn is over and she does not win the pot.

Lingo

High Roller–player who rolls the highest amount

First Shooter–the player who rolls first

Pot–collected chips that will be distributed to the winner

Snake Eyes–a roll of two ones

Boxcars–a roll of two sixes

Each player rolls one die to determine who will go first in the game. The high roller is the first shooter.

Object

To roll lucky numbers so that you collect more counters than your opponents.

How to Play

1. Each player puts a counter in the "pot."

2. The first shooter rolls the dice and either wins the pot with a throw specified above or loses his turn. If he wins the pot, all players put in another counter for the next round of the game. If the player loses his turn, the pot remains where it is and play passes to the next player.

3. A winning shooter gets to collect the pot and keep the dice to roll first in the next round of the game.

MAKE YOUR OWN DECK

Encourage players to help their friends by sharing items that might be appropriate to another child's topic.

K-4 • Group • Recognition/Cut and Paste • Hands-On • Medium • Cooperation

Materials

index cards
magazines
pair of scissors per
    child
glue

Get Started

Provide children with index cards, scissors, magazines and glue. Assign children various topics to find in their magazines. There should be two cards for every object or subject. When children have found the particular picture, it is pasted on an index card.

Encourage players to help their friends by sharing items that might be appropriate to another child's topic.

Object

To have your own homemade deck of cards.

Variations

- The cards can relate to various themes: farm, pets, wildlife, nature, transportation, household items, health and fitness or any other curriculum-related topic.

- Once the picture cards have been made, print the word of the item to help early readers with word recognition and reading skills.

- Cards can be made to have numerals and matching visuals, upper and lowercase letters of the alphabet, a word and a matching picture, a color and the color word and so on depending upon the particular age group.

MEMORY MATCH WITH YOUR OWN DECK

Materials

your own home-
made deck of
cards
flat playing sur-
face

K-4 • Two to Four • Recognition/Memory/Matching • Hands-On • Medium-Long

Get Started

Shuffle the deck and have players lay the cards down on the
playing surface, near but not
touching one another. Cards can
be laid in straight rows, in a random manner or in a circular fan
pattern.

Object

To match and acquire more pairs of cards than the other players.

How to Play

1. The first player turns over one card and then another, revealing the
   faces for all to see. If the cards match (i.e., two threes, two kings, etc.),
   the player may keep that pair and go on to select another two cards.
   This player continues until she turns over two cards that do not match.
   When two unmatched cards are turned over, they are replaced (face-
   down) in the exact spots where they were first touched. Play then
   passes to the player to the left or right.

2. The next player reveals two cards and so on. The game continues in
   this manner until all of the pairs have been united.

3. Players count the number of pairs they have collected in the game. The
   player with the most pairs wins the game.

Variations

COOPERATIVE CONCENTRATION

This game follows the same basic structure of Concentration.

- Players turn cards over to make matches, but in this game children
  may help each other in the hunt for pairs.

- One player is designated as The Keeper. All matched pairs are given
  to The Keeper. With each new pair, The Keeper announces how many
  pairs have been collected.

- The object of the game is to collect 15 pairs before a designated time
  has elapsed.

CREATIVE CONCENTRATION

Turn an art project into a game of Concentration. Paint stones, the bottom
of bottle caps, beans or clay markers for a game of Concentration.

SHUFFLE THOSE CARDS

Collect cards brought in from home in a basket.

K-4 • Two or More • Math • Hands-On • Short-Long

CARD FREE PLAY

Leave the basket at a center during activity times and see what kids come up with all on their own.

- What do kids notice about the cards? Designs? Numbers? Symbols? Do they use the backs as well as the faces in their games?

- Find out what games kids already know.

- Make card houses.

CARD TASKS

Once kids have experienced the cards through free play, introduce some activities. Begin with a deck of aces, twos and threes for beginners. Introduce more cards as the skills improve.

- Count the cards in today's basket.

- How many more cards do you need to make up a deck? Is this a full deck? Two decks?

- How many should you throw away or do you need to make it a proper deck? How many of each card are there in a proper deck?

ORGANIZING TASKS

- Arrange the cards from the highest value to the lowest.

- Arrange the cards in numbered groups of four.

- Sort the cards by suit.

- Sort the cards by color.

TWO-CARD MATH DRAW

- Use the cards for subtraction and multiplication exercises.

- Pull two cards from the basket. What is the sum of these two cards?

- Pull two cards from the basket. Subtract the lesser amount from the greater amount. What is your _____?

- Pull two cards from the deck. Multiply these together. What is the product? If a player gets the correct answer, they may keep the cards; if a player gets a wrong answer, the cards are shuffled back into the deck.

NUMBER STORIES

- Make up and record addition and subtraction stories using the basket and the cards.

SNAP

Materials

1 or 2 decks of cards
flat playing surface

Snap!

Get Started

Choose one player to "deal" the cards. Distribute the entire deck among the players.

Object

To collect all of the cards.

How to Play

1. When the cards have been dealt, the first player puts one card faceup on the playing surface.

2. The second player puts a card on top, faceup and then the third player and so on.

3. At anytime, if a card that is placed down has the same numerical or face value as the previous card laid, any player in the game may call "Snap" and slap their hand over the pile of cards. The first player to cover the deck with her hand collects the card pile. These cards are added to her hand to be used in play.

4. Play continues in this manner and players are eliminated as they run out of cards. The game ends when one player has collected all of the cards and all other players have been eliminated.

ADD TO 21

3-4 • Two to Four • Adding/Strategy/Analysis • Hands-On • Short-Medium

Get Started

Choose one player to be the dealer.

Object

To be the player whose cards equal or are the closest to 21 without going over 21.

How to Play

1. The dealer hands each player two cards.

2. Each player adds these cards together to determine the sum of his hand. Face cards are worth 10; the ace is worth one.

3. In turn the dealer will ask each player if they would like another card. The dealer will continue to ask a player who is taking cards.

4. When all players have either chosen to hold or have folded, then players will reveal their sums.

5. The player with the sum closest to 21 is the winner.

Strategy

- A player who has a sum considerably below 21 will have to make a decision to take a card or stay at the particular sum. Players may choose to take risks to get closer to 21 or hold at a lower number hoping that the other players will end up with a sum higher than 21 or a sum lower than that of the particular hand.

SHUFFLE MATH

2-4 • Two • Addition/Fine Motor Skills • Hands-On • Medium-Long

Materials

ruler
pencil and marker
24" x 32" (60 x 80 cm) piece of tagboard or other sturdy material
4 to 8 coins

Get Started

MAKE THE SHUFFLEBOARD

1. Using a ruler, draw the base of a triangle on one end of the cardboard piece.
2. Draw two lines that join at a point in the middle of the other end of the cardboard.
3. Divide that triangle into sections as shown.
4. Use your marker to indicate the point values ranging from 5 to 25. Include two ones for coins that miss the target.
5. Draw a line 2" (5 cm) from the other end of the board. Players cannot cross that line with any part of their body when they shuffle their coin across.

DIAGRAM OF SHUFFLEBOARD

Provide each player with two coins or playing pieces. Decide which player will go first.

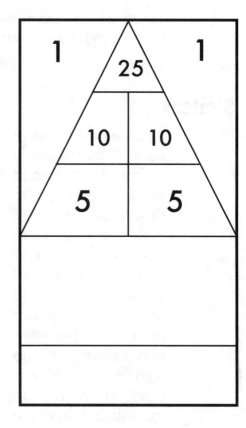

How to Play

1. Place the board on a flat playing surface.
2. In turn, players shuffle their coins across the starting line towards the the triangular scoring area. A player may knock the other player's coin out of the target or into the 1 sections. Try not to knock your own piece out of the game.
3. Players collect their coins and keep a tally of their points until one player reaches 100 points.

Variation

- Make up your own number scheme that reflects the current math concepts being taught in your class. Try using fractions, decimals, negative numbers or a number currently being multiplied (for example, use fives, ones and zeros if you are learning the multiplication facts).

60

NUMBER GUESS

This games takes a lot of concentration!

3-4 • Pairs • Adding/Coordination • Hands-On • Short

Get Started

Limber up those fingers!

How to Play

1. Players begin by counting "one, two, three" together. On the count of three they throw their right hand forward with a number of fingers extended. At the same time each player calls out a number they think might be the sum of the extended fingers. If the number called by one of the players is in fact the sum of the extended fingers of both players, the player who called the correct number gets a point.

2. Play continues until one of the players reaches a specified number of points.

MARBLE MATH

K-4 • Any Number • Manual Dexterity/Addition • Mild Activity • Medium

Get Started

MAKE THE MARBLE MATH BOX

1. Remove the box lid and turn the box upside down. Decide which side will be the target face of the box.

2. Use your marker to draw three to five marble tunnels as shown in the diagram.

3. Cut out the marked areas to make your marble tunnels. Mark high numbers above the smaller tunnels and small numbers above the larger tunnels. (Use numbers that are relevant to your current math program. For example, 1 to 10 or multiples of a current multiplication fact you are studying.)

4. Set the board up in front of a wall or other barrier.

5. Mark a fair shooting line about 3 feet (1 m) from the box.

6. Decide upon a point score that will make one player a winner.

7. Provide each player with 5 to 10 marbles or divide the bag of marbles equally among players. (This could be a math lesson in itself!)

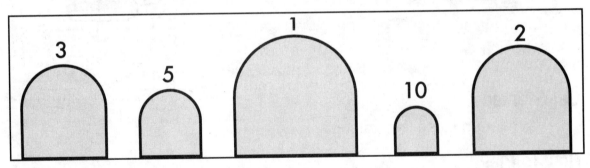

Object

Players attempt to get their marbles through the tunnels and score the most points, being the first player to reach a designated score.

How to Play

1. Place the box against a wall or backboard of some type. Set the box so the doors are facing the players.

2. Players take turns shooting one marble at a time, attempting to get their marbles through the tunnels so they can collect points.

3. Players can keep a written point tally or add in their heads and help one another to keep their scores straight.

4. The winner is the first player to reach the designated score or the player with the highest score after all marbles have been shot.

MINUTE MATH ACTIVITIES

K-3 • Two or More • Math Skill Reinforcement • Mild Activity • Short-Medium

Get Started

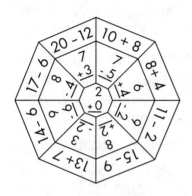

Draw a target of some sort on the chalkboard. Within each area of the target write a number, letter, word or color to be identified or a math or written problem to be solved or a question to be answered. Consider the following designs for your simple targets:

The most difficult area of the target to hit (usually the smallest area) should hold the simplest problem. The larger areas should contain the more difficult problems.

Establish a throwing line about 10 feet (3.1 m) from the board–base the distance placement of this line on the accuracy of the throws for your particular group. Select a child to throw first. Wet the sponge ball with water. It should be damp, not soaking wet.

Materials

chalkboard
chalk
wet sponge ball

How to Play

1. Have the player stand at the throwing line and throw the wet ball towards the target on the chalkboard.

2. Where the ball hits the target will be marked with a water spot. The player must reveal the number, letter, color, solve the problem or answer the question within the area her ball hit.

3. A child who answers the question or identifies the specified letter, color or word will be awarded a bean or other counter.

4. If there is a small group, play will rotate among players. If there are more than five players, the group should be divided into teams and play will go back and forth between teams. Any counters earned will be placed in the team's cup.

5. The game will end at a specified time. At this time the players or teams will count their beans. The player or team with the most beans wins.

TRADING

An ancient game that really needs no introduction!

1-4 • Group • Concept Building • Hands-On • Cooperative

In the past people often traded items they grew, made or owned for things that they needed. This trading of goods is known as the barter system. People could pay for milk with eggs or buy a chair in exchange for hours of labor in the field. People realized that it was easier to trade metal coins and paper bills than cows and bales of straw. In time most societies developed a form of currency used in exchange for items. Today we trade our services and goods for currency and then use this currency to pay for things we need or want. Each country has its own form of money. In the United States, Canada and Australia, dollars are used. In Sweden it's the krona, Italy the lira, Japan the yen, Portugal the escudo . . . you get the idea!

From marbles, sports cards and hockey shirts to labor, money, stocks and bonds, trading goes on everywhere. Entire societies have been structured around their systems of trading. Children are well aware of this process at an early age.

Kids' natural interest in trading can teach them about analysis, counting, tallying and strategies used to acquire something desirable and effective communication skills. An educator or parent can help to provide assistance in these early trades where kids can learn about decision making, fairness and saying "no."

Trading can be used in many valuable lessons. Try these arenas of trade:

CLASSROOM TOY EXCHANGE

Help the environment and foster some negotiation skills with this exchange activity. Send a note home with children requesting that some outgrown toys be brought in for the Classroom Toy Exchange. Children can barter directly and trade or can be given tokens for items based on their value. Children will then trade tokens for new items of interest. Sound familiar?

It's a good idea to have a few extra toys on hand for those who are not able to bring in exchange material for tokens.

TRADING DAY

Allow children to exchange sports cards, marbles, POGs or other valued items during class time. Talk about why some items are valued more than others, ways to acquire the desirable items and rules of fair trade.

FAIR TRADE

Have each student prepare a chart with two columns. The first column heading will read: "Things I Need or Want" and the second will read: "What I Could Trade." Children will record items they need or want and then think about items or services they could trade with parents or friends to help them acquire the items. Is the exchange of goods and services a fair trade?

64

TRADING COLORS

1-4 • Group • Problem Solving • Mild Activity • Medium • Cooperation

Get Started

Provide each child with six tokens taken randomly from the bowl.

Materials

set of red, orange, yellow, green, blue, violet tokens for each person in the group

Object

To trade your tokens until you have one complete "rainbow."

How to Play

1. Once each child has been provided with six tokens, they are allowed to mingle with one another.

2. Players will move around the room asking other players if they have or need a particular color. Players trade one color for another but are not allowed to give tokens away. Players must have six tokens at all times.

3. The game is over when all players have a complete rainbow.

Variations

- Once players have learned to play the game, they can race against time. Try to trade for rainbows within five minutes, then two. It's a wonderful way to encourage cooperation and strategic thought.

- Instead of trading for rainbows, players could trade for a set of numbers, letters to spell a word, farm animals or other topics related to a relevant concept.

DOMINOES

K-4 • Two to Four • Matching/Strategy/Problem Solving • Hands-On

Materials

set of 28 "bones" or dominoes
flat playing surface

These simple black blocks with white dots are useful teaching aids to introduce children to numbers, number concepts, counting, matching and adding. Dominoes were invented by the Chinese at least 300 years ago and spread into Europe through Italy in the eighteenth century. Early dominoes were made of thin pieces of bone–then ebony and bone, then black stained wood and today plastic. The game described is the European version of this popular game.

Get Started

Place the dominoes face-down on the flat surface. Have each player choose seven dominoes from the "bone yard" and place them on one edge so the face is visible only to the player who chose them.

Blank tiles or ends are considered wild and can represent any number.

How to Play

1. The first player lays any domino from his tiles faceup on the playing surface.

2. Play moves in a clockwise fashion, to the next player who matches one end of the laid domino with one end of her own. If she cannot match a piece, she may pick from the bone yard. If this piece can be played, it is laid before the next player's turn. If the piece cannot be played, it is added to the player's row for future placing and another is drawn and another until one domino can be played or there are only two bones remaining in the bone yard. Play then passes to the next player.

3. The next player must match a corresponding end to one of the laid pieces and so on until one player has used up all of her dominoes.

4. When the game ends, players turn their remaining pieces faceup. The sum of the remaining dominoes is the score given to the winning player. This score is recorded and players prepare for another round.

5. The first player to reach a score of 200 is the winner.

Variation
FOUR-PLAYER DOMINOES

This game is played as above but without the "bone yard." The player who chooses the double six leads the game. In the event of a stale game, where no tiles can be laid, the tiles are all turned over. The player with the lowest sum is declared the winner. His points are subtracted from the total sum of points of all of the players to determine his score. If a player cannot match one end of the domino to the pieces on the game, he will call, "pass," and play will proceed to the next player.

COOPERATIVE DOMINOES

This cooperative version makes dominoes fun for even the youngest players!

K-1 • Two to Four • Game Playing/Matching/Counting/Numeral Recognition
Hands-On • Medium • Cooperative

Get Started

Players familiarize themselves with the tiles. They count them together, look at the formations and place some with the same number or dots side by side. In this game the blank tile counts as zero or nothing. When children are familiar with the faces of the dominoes, the dominoes are turned facedown. Each child selects five tiles which they place faceup in front of themselves. One tile is selected and placed faceup on the playing surface. The remaining tiles are left facedown in the "pool" or "bone yard."

Object

To place as many tiles as possible in the domino formation.

How to Play

1. The first player surveys his tiles to see if he can match one end with one of the tile ends in the playing area. Other players may assist if needed. If the player finds a tile that can be placed, it is added to the appropriate end of the domino chain. If he does not find a matching tile, then he may take a tile from the pool, which can be added to the chain if possible and play passes to the next player. Whenever a player adds a tile to the game, a new tile is taken from the pool.

2. The second player takes a turn as above and so on until all of the tiles that can be, have been added to the chain and all of the players have won!

Variation

• Players can add dominoes in a manner that causes the domino chain to twist and turn as long as the matching ends are placed side by side.

DOMINO BUILDING

It's delicate work that takes a steady hand. Try making patterns or setting up lines of dominoes that can be knocked down for a spectacular effect.

TANGRAM

1-4 • One • Creativity/Problem Solving/Spatial Abilities • Hands-On

This game originated in China about the early 1800s and quickly spread around the world. There are at least 1,600 possible designs to be made with the seven pieces.

MAKE YOUR OWN TANGRAM

Photocopy the accompanying tangram onto sturdy construction paper or have children glue a copied tangram to a piece of stiff tagboard. Cut the seven tans and prepare to test imaginations and perseverance!

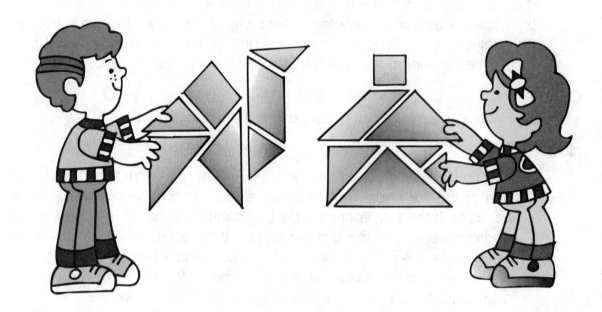

Object

To create your own designs or duplicate given silhouettes using the seven tans.

How to Play

Create your own designs.

Have children arrange the pieces to form silhouettes of geometrical shapes, creatures, people or other objects. Allow the children to suggest objects for everyone to try to make. Provide children with paper to draw their solutions.

Duplicate a shape from its silhouette.

Provide the students with shape silhouettes or tracings. Have them try to make identical shapes.

Use the tangram as a tool to help teach geometry.

This geometrical puzzle makes a great tool to help teach geometry. See the accompanying sheet (page 70).

TANGRAM DIAGRAM

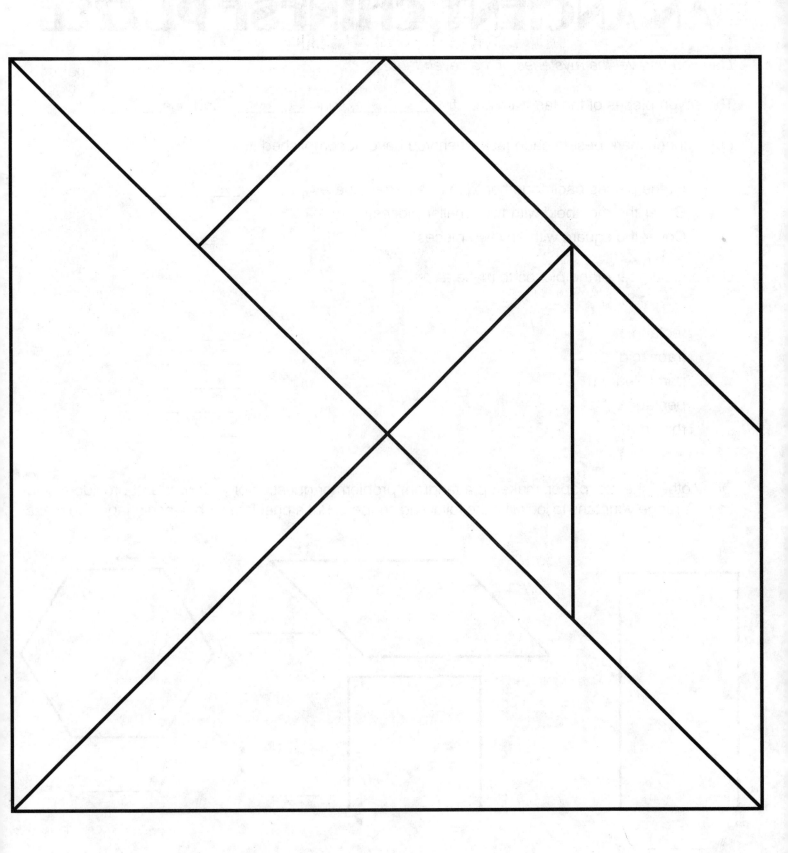

Name _____

THE TANGRAM
AN ANCIENT CHINESE PUZZLE

Can you unravel the mysteries of the seven tans?

The seven pieces of the tangram are: five _____, one _____ and one _____.

Put a check mark beside each task when you have accomplished it.

      Fit the pieces back together to form a large square.   _____

      Cover the rhomboid with two smaller pieces.   _____

      Cover the square with any two pieces.   _____

Use any number of the pieces to make a . . .

      rectangle   _____

      trapezoid   _____

      parallelogram   _____

      pentagon   _____

      rhombus   _____

On another sheet of paper, make up a tangram problem or question of your own and provide a solution. Arrange your tans to look like the following shapes. Put a check mark by each shape you make.

MATH TOSS

K-4 • Group • Math Facts • Mild Activity • Short-Medium

Get Started

Choose a math skill you would like to work on with your particular group– counting, counting by a particular number, multiplication, patterning, etc. Make children aware of what information you will be seeking and how many seconds they will be allowed before they must return the beanbag.

How to Play

1. Call out a number to be followed up with the next number, a pattern to be continued or a multiplication question to be answered and then throw the beanbag to a player. For example, the leader may call out, "2 x 4," and toss the bag.

2. The player must catch the beanbag, respond and return the beanbag to the leader.

3. If the child answers cor- rectly, a new question or continuation is added and the beanbag is tossed again. If the question is not answered correctly, it is repeated until a correct response is given.

Variation

• This game may also be played with a ball, allowing for one or no bounces before an answer is given.

Materials

beanbag

2x4

12 UP

3-4 • Two • Addition/Problem Solving/Strategy • Hands-On • Medium

Materials

egg carton or other surface with 12 depressions in it
1 set of dice
pebbles or marbles

Get Started

Number the depressions from 1 to 12. Determine which player is to roll the dice first and begin the game!

Object

To place the markers in the depressions in a way in which you gain the highest number of points.

How to Play

1. The first player rolls the dice and determines the sum of the dice. She places her tokens in the numbered holes in a way that will equal the sum of the dice. (For example, if the player rolls the sum of 8, she will put one token in the number 8 or if the 8 is already filled, a combination of numbers that will equal 8 [1 and 7 or 2 and 6 or 3 and 5]) When the exact number is filled, a combination of numbers may be filled.

2. This player continues to roll the dice and place her markers until all 12 counters are placed or until she is "stumped," meaning all of the depressions that can make up a particular sum are filled.

3. When a player's turn has ended, she may add the numbers in which she has placed her tokens. She must subtract the number of tokens she has left from her total score.

4. Play then moves to the second player who rolls the dice and places tokens in the same manner.

5. The game may end after each player has had one or two turns or when one player reaches a designated point score (usually 25 or 50).

Strategy

• Players attempt to keep the smaller numbers free for combinations.

MATCH THE MEASUREMENT

1-4 • Group • Estimation and Measurement • Hands-On • Medium

Get Started

Have each child stand against a wall and have a piece of masking tape placed on the wall to represent their height. Number each piece of masking tape and record the number and the player's name on a master sheet. Players must not tell others their number.

Object

To determine which players are represented by which numbered measurement marks on the wall.

How to Play

1. When all players have had their height taped to the wall, all players are given paper and pencil and asked to match the number on each tape with a member of the group.

2. Players may walk around and study the marks and the other players before writing a name with each number on their page.

3. When all players have completed their measurement match guesses, the identity of each number is revealed.

4. Players mark their guesses as the identities are revealed. The player with the most correct guesses is the winner.

UP THE WALL

2-4 • Pairs • Measurement/Problem Solving • Active • Medium • Cooperative

Materials

masking tape
a wall
measuring instrument (ruler or tape)
chalkboard or master list for recorded measurements

Get Started

Have the players form pairs.

Object

To jump higher than any other player.

How to Play

1. Partners take turns standing flat-footed beside the wall and stretching their hand as high up the wall as they can. The spot they reach is marked with chalk or masking tape on the wall. The other partner may need to stand on a chair to mark this height accurately.

2. Players measure the distance of this reach from the floor and record it on a master list.

3. When all players have had an opportunity to stretch, mark the wall and measure, the second part of this activity is explained.

4. Partners take turns, one standing on a chair to mark the next measurement and the other taking a jump as high as he can to reach a spot higher than the previous mark.

5. Players measure and record this new height.

6. Each player now must determine how high they jumped. This is done by measuring the distance between the first and second marks. Record this in the third column of the master list.

7. The player who jumped the highest is the winner.

Variations

• Graph the statistics in various ways.

GUESS HOW MANY

A guessing game that brightens your room and builds math skills, too!

K-4 • Any Number • Estimating • Sedentary • Short • Cooperative

Get Started

Put the container in a spot where it is visible to all children. Change the contents on a regular basis for new estimating challenges.

Object

To guess the correct number of items in the container.

How to Play

1. Encourage children to analyze the contents of the container using only their eyes.

2. Some time during the month children record their estimates and place in a box or write them on a chart provided beside the container.

3. On the last day of the month the contents of the jar is counted by the leader or as a group math activity.

4. The player who guesses closest to the actual amount is the winner and shares her guessing technique and (if appropriate) the contents of the container.

Materials

large see-through container
interesting items to fill the container on a monthly basis – consider acorns, buttons, marbles, gum balls, jelly beans, dried beans, lollipops, Easter eggs, Christmas balls, wooden blocks, paper clips and so on
ballot box and papers or guessing chart and pen

Variations

- Extend this game to include discussions of the strategies used by various children. What seems to work? What doesn't? Kids can share their guessing techniques.

- This game may present opportunities to discuss interaction skills. Players should be encouraged to respect all guesses . . . and all other guessers.

MATH RACE

1-3 • Any Number • Mathematical Drill • Sedentary • Medium

Materials

chalkboard and chalk

covering for the chalkboard (tape and paper or pull down screen)

1 Indy 500 Racetrack page for each participant

set of dice

timer

Get Started

Write a series of problems on the chalkboard. If possible, cover these to keep them out of sight of the players. Or write the problems on a piece of bristol board that can be presented at the appropriate time. Each player is provided with a file folder or a folded piece of 16" x 20" (41 x 51 cm) construction paper. On the inside right-hand side, the player will paste the Indy 500 Racetrack page. Children may color this page.

Object

Players will attempt to finish the car race ahead of their opponent–the dice.

How to Play

1. When the problems are revealed, all participants will mentally solve the problems and record only the answer on their papers.

2. When the allotted time has elapsed, the leader or teacher will ring the bell to signal all participants to stop solving and writing.

3. Answers to each question will be taken up and recorded on the board. Players will allot themselves one mile/kilometer for every correct answer. She will color in the corresponding number of blocks on the racetrack in her lane. If a child received seven correct answers, then the child may proceed ahead seven spaces by marking or coloring each mile covered.

4. The dice will be rolled by a chosen "driver" to determine the number of miles/kilometers the opponent's car may travel. All players will be playing against the same roll of the dice. Players color the correct number of blocks in the opponent's lane.

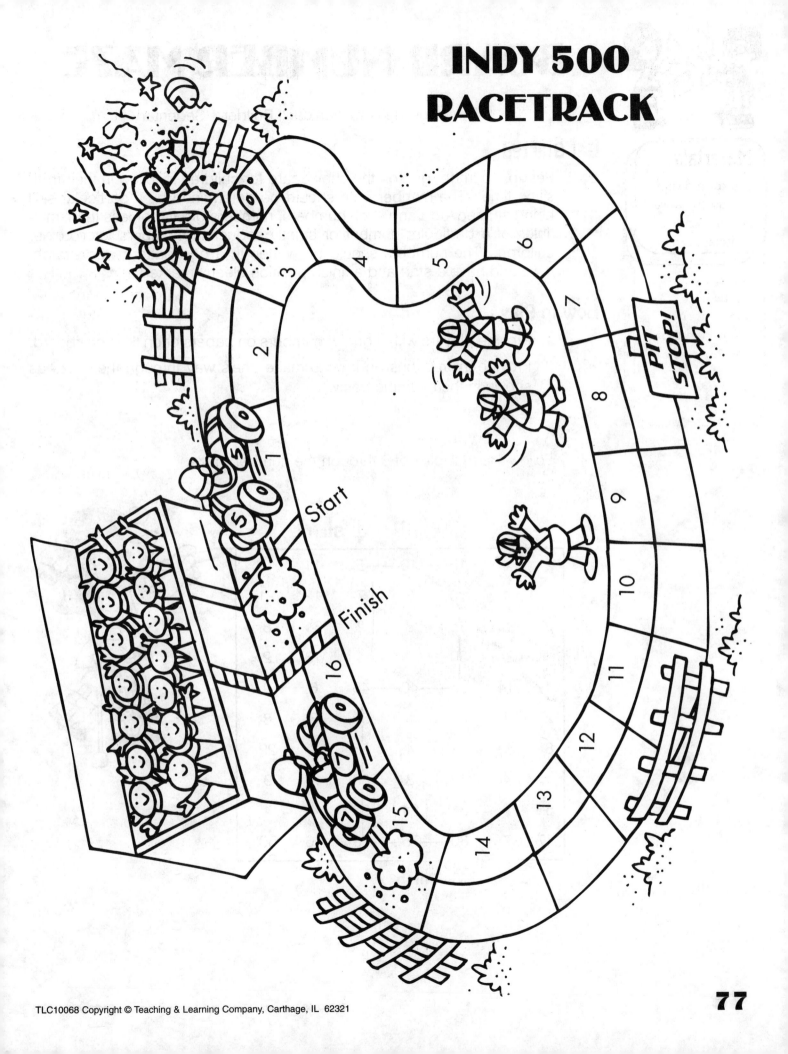

INDY 500 RACETRACK

Start

Finish

PIT STOP!

1 2 3 4 5 6 7 8 9 10 11 12 13 14 15 16

BOARD NUMBER MAZE

1-4 • One • Mathematical Skill Builder • Sedentary

Materials

chalkboard and chalk (or white board and markers)

Get Started

Set up a number grid on the chalkboard for children to follow in their transition time. The number path should be determined by a particular skill being studied—odd and even numbers, numbers greater or less than, multiples of a particular number or strictly sequential numbers for younger children. The numbers should be written in a grid pattern with straight rows and have a start and a finish position clearly marked.

How to Play

1. Provide players with a grid of numbers on papers or on the chalkboard.
2. Provide instructions on how to make one's way through the maze as shown in the example below.

Follow the multiples of 5 through the number maze.

↓ **Start**

2	4	15——10——5	11	14
3	1	20	3	7	12	21
9	29	25	8	2	31	3
11	22	30	7	4	18	2
19	14	35——40——45	6	9
27	1	26	3	50	3	8
8	23	21	4	55	3	29
13	4	12	8	60	16	9
6	3	31	24	65	4	4
17	7	80——75——70	16	50

↑ **Finish**

PROBLEMS AND MYSTERIES EVERYWHERE

Intellectual challenges encourage children to stretch their mental capabilities and discover the cognitive talents they possess. The games in this chapter challenge young learners to think creatively, develop newly acquired skills and practice problem solving.

WHAT DID YOU SEE?

K-4 • Group • Recall/Observation • Sedentary • Short

Object

To recall items viewed.

How to Play

1. The teacher or leader places 5 to 40 items on a desktop and covers them so children cannot see them. This is best done in the morning before children arrive or at some point when children are out of the room. The number of items depends upon the grade level. Always start with a number of items that will allow for reasonable success for the group and then work up to a greater number as children develop skills of observation and recall.

2. When children are seated and prepared to look, uncover the items for about 20 seconds.

3. Cover the items again and ask children to recall what they saw. These recollections can be written on individual pieces of paper or shared verbally with the group.

Materials

5 to 40 interesting
   items
cloth covering
table
timing device

THE MATCHING GAME

The Matching Board allows you to make a game of almost any skill or fact and help to reinforce it.

2-3 • One to Two • Skill Reinforcement • Hands-On • Short-Medium

Materials

sturdy cardboard
paper fasteners
2 3" to 5" (7 to
    12 cm) pieces of
    dowelling
electrical tape
thin wire
1.5-volt battery
    (AA, C or D cell)
1.5 to 3.0-volt
    flashlight battery
light bulb
bulb holder (found
    at an electronics
    dealer)
adhesive Velcro™
    strips or Velcro™
    strips and glue
tagboard
colorful markers
photos or maga-
    zine pictures
    (optional)
laminate (optional)

Get Started

MAKE A MATCHING BOARD

1. Draw one column down the left and right side of the board.
2. Punch or mark a row with an equal number of holes down each column.
3. Attach a paper fastener in each hole.
4. Attach Velcro™ strips beside each paper fastener in both columns.
5. On the back of the cardboard, wrap the bare ends of the wire around the paper fasteners to connect each word to the corresponding picture.
6. Connect a wire from one terminal of the battery to one screw on the bulb holder.
7. Connect a long wire from the other screw on the light bulb holder to a dowel. Tape the wire to the dowel with a small section of wire exposed at the end of the dowel to act as a pointer wand. Touch the dowel ends together to test your circuit.
8. Attach one end of the third wire to the battery terminal and the other end to the other dowel.
9. Touch one dowel to a paper fastener in one column and the other dowel to a paper fastener in the other column. The appropriate picture-to-word match will allow the bulb to light.

Prepare the Match Cards

1. Prepare tagboard tag sets for the various games. If you have four sets of fasteners, prepare a set of four matching tags.

2. Attach the opposing Velcro™ piece to the back of the tags. (If possible, laminate the tags first for greater durability.)

Consider the following matching tags for educational games:

I Know My Numbers: Numerals and corresponding pictorial representations. Consider hot gluing beans or using stickers for effect.

Alphabet Fun: Corresponding upper and lowercase letters

Learn-to-Read Match Game: Photos, drawings or magazine pictures and corresponding words in print

Fraction Match: Numerical fraction and corresponding pictorial representations

Number Facts: Addition, subtraction or multiplication problems and corresponding sums and products

World Traveler: Map segments and location names

Bilingual Match: Corresponding words in two languages

Create your own tag sets using other relevant topics with matching possibilities. Put each tag set in a separate box, sealed plastic bag or envelope.

Prepare the Board for Play

Choose one fact set and fasten the Velcro™ tags on the Velcro™ columns. Place one set of data in one column and the corresponding match information in a random pattern in the other column.

How to Play

1. A player takes one wand in one hand and one in the other and attempts to match the corresponding segment of information, i.e. the two matching tags.

2. When a correct match is made, the light provides instant response to a correct match. If the light does not come on, the child will know that the match is not correct and may try again. A child may play until he has mastered all of the facts on the match board.

I LOVE TO EAT

This puzzling little game will keep players' minds active for some time.

2-4 • Two or More • Pattern Recognition/Analysis/Language • Sedentary • Short-Long

Get Started

Select one player to be the leader.

Object

To determine the rule or gimmick being used by the leader.

How to Play

1. The leader announces, "I like to eat _____ but not _____." The leader chooses a criterion known only to herself, which determines her likes and dislikes. It may be that the food must start with a particular letter or with the last letter of the previous player's favorite food. The food may need to be a vegetable or a breakfast food or any other reasonable rule.

2. The second player says, "You like to eat _____." The leader answers, "Yes I do like to eat _____" or "No I do not like to eat _____" as another clue to help players figure out the gimmick.

3. After each player's turn, the leader reveals one more item she likes to eat.

4. The game continues until a player figures out the rule and reveals it to others.

5. The player who solved the puzzle becomes the leader for another round.

Variations

- Modify the game to meet a particular theme being studied: I travel on a _____, I want to go to _____, I like the number _____ or any other variation that fits your group.

WHAT IF?

This simple opening line can open minds to new possibilities.

K-4 • Group • Creativity • Sedentary • Short-Medium • Cooperative

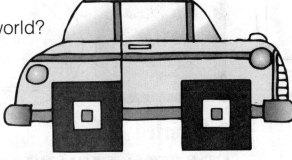

Get Started

Pose a "what if . . . " question. Try these for starters:

What if . . .

Humans could fly?

Cars had square wheels?

There was no electricity?

There were no colors in the world?

The oceans were boiling?

Ants wore pants?

The world was flat?

and so on!

Object

To think creatively about "what ifs."

How to Play

Have children verbally discuss the question, draw pictures or write their thoughts on paper or the chalkboard.

Variations

- Have children respond in print or drawing on a large piece of mural paper for an open house display.

- Let kids invent their own "what ifs"–the questions can be as creative as the answers.

83

SIGNS, SIGNS, SIGNS

This tricky little game keeps minds working!

2-4 • Two or More • Symbol and Word Recognition/Creativity • Hands-On • Long

Materials

magazines, news-
papers, pam-
phlets, photo-
graphs
scissors
chalkboard, bul-
letin board or
other display
surface

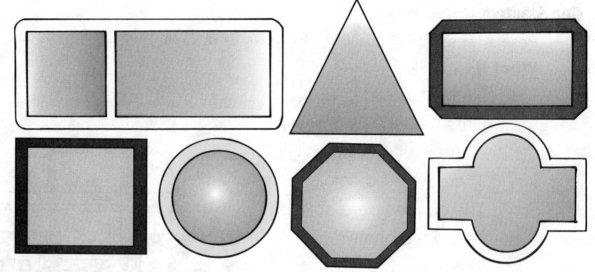

Get Started

CREATE A SIGN WALL!

Cut interesting signs from magazines, newspapers or pamphlets. Take photos of interesting signs. Paste the signs to the sign board (chalkboard) with space under each for children's interpretations of the signs. Ask children to create their own signs or contribute pictures of interesting ones they have found to the sign wall.

How to Play

1. Participants can study the signs and then write what they think each sign means on the paper under the sign. The collection of guessed meanings becomes part of the Sign Wall's appeal!

   or

   Number each sign and provide paper for each participant. Participants write the number of the sign and what they think is the meaning of that sign on their paper.

2. The player who guesses the correct meanings of the most signs wins.

Variations

- Take a sign hunt around the school. Have participants record the signs they see.

- Talk about the role signs play in our lives.

- How does our ability to read affect the effectiveness of signs?

- Why are symbols useful?

- Make some signs of your own.

RUBBINGS

K-4 • Any Number • Art/Visual Discrimination/Observation • Hands-On • Medium-Long

Materials

thin paper (typing, tracing or newsprint will do)

dark crayons, pencils or charcoal with flat sides

Get Started

Have children take their paper and rubbing material on a texture hike around the school or classroom. Each child should make four rubbings. This is done by placing the paper on a surface, holding it firmly in place and rubbing the flat side of their marking instrument back and forth to make an impression of the textured surface. Completed papers are signed and taped to a "viewing wall."

How to Play

1. When all participants' rubbings have been taped to the viewing area, the fun can begin.

2. One at a time, children come to the viewing area and identify the subject of a particular rubbing. If the child is correct, she takes that rubbing back to her desk. If the child has guessed incorrectly, she sits down and must try to guess a different rubbing on her next turn.

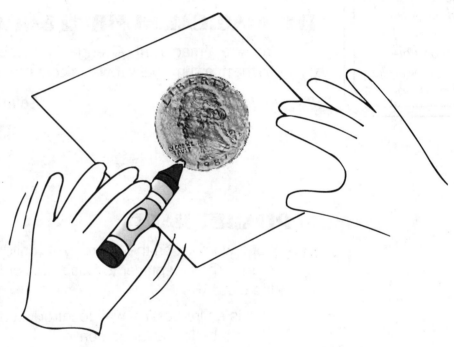

3. The guessing continues in this manner until each child has claimed one rubbing.

4. In turn, children will have the opportunity to guess the subject of the remaining rubbings. As the remaining rubbings will become increasingly more difficult to identify, a player may choose to pass.

5. The game continues until all of the rubbings have been identified and claimed or the few remaining rubbings cannot be identified.

6. Players now count the number of rubbings they were able to "claim." The player with the most is rewarded for having such a discriminating eye!

7. Each player collects their own rubbings to frame with construction paper and hang on their wall.

CHALKBOARD CHALLENGES

Keep kids puzzling all day long with clever quips, puzzles and problems prepared on the chalkboard and ready each morning to be tackled by students who complete all of their work or arrive early in the classroom and are looking for intellectual challenge.

2-4 • Any Number • Cognitive • Sedentary • Short

INTERSECTION PUZZLE

Put the numbers 1, 2, 3, 4, 5, 6 and 7 in the sections of the interlocking circles so that the sum of the numbers in each circle is the same. (You can put in the numbers 1, 4 and 6)

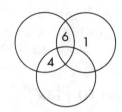

THE MAGICAL NUMBER SQUARE

You are a magician! Arrange the numbers from 1 to 9 in a magical square so that the sum of any row–horizontal, diagonal or vertical–will always total 15.

Solution

4	9	2
3	5	7
8	1	6

ALPHABET RACE

Put a word list on the board. Ask children to put the words in alphabetical order. The first player to finish wins or if the entire class "beats the clock," the class wins.

This is an interesting way to introduce the spelling list, new words or skills of alphabetical arrangement.

HOW LONG IS A PIECE OF STRING?

Twice the distance from the middle to the end.

ADD FIVE LINES TO SIX TO GET NINE

/ / / / / / *becomes* N I N E

Variation

* Provide some space on the chalkboard for children to share their own puzzles with solutions readily available.

SQUARE DESIGNS

Using only straight lines, connect some or all of the dots. Can you make a different design in each square?

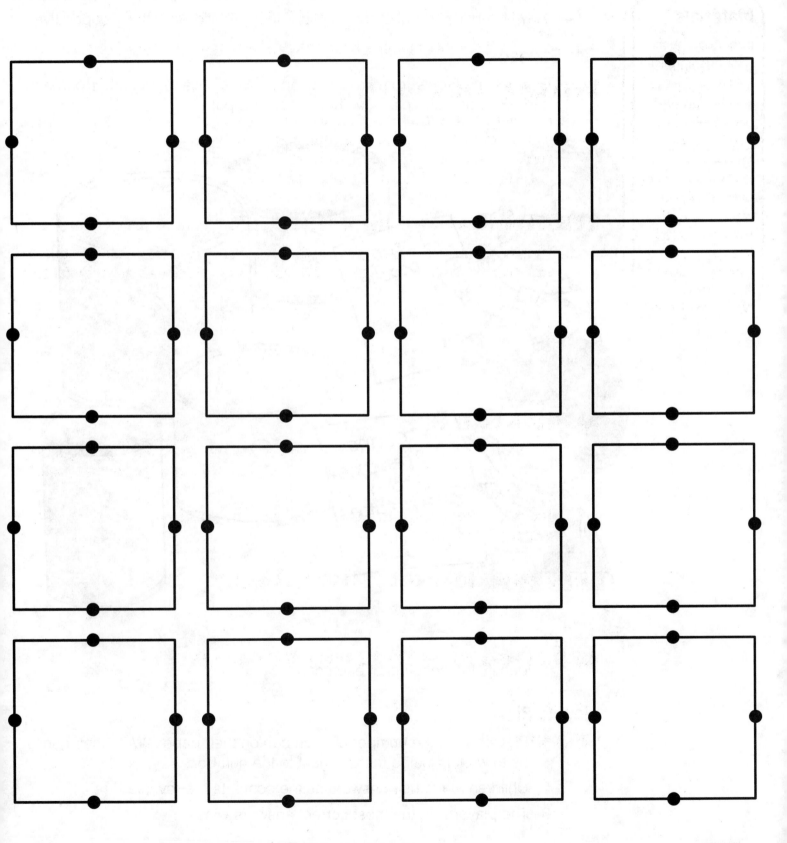

CAN YOU NAME THAT CAN?

Materials

paper and pencil for each participant
variety of interesting shaped tin cans

Get Started

Remove the labels from various shaped cans. Place a number on each can. Provide each player with a pencil and paper.

Object

To identify the contents of each can.

How to Play

1. Players write the number of each can on their paper. Write their guess as to what is inside the can next to the number.

2. Children mark their answers as the contents are revealed.

3. The player with the most correct answers wins.

WHAT IS IT?

1-4 • Any Number • Creative Analysis/Problem Solving • Mild Activity • Medium

Get Started

Set up a display of interesting pioneer and modern tools, gadgets and novelty items. Place a number on or beside each item.

Object

To determine the purpose or function of each item.

How to Play

1. Provide each participant with pencil and paper and allow them to walk carefully and observe the items on display.

2. Each participant records the number of each item on their paper and their independent guess regarding the possible function or name of the item.

3. When all players have recorded the item numbers and their guesses, you can reveal the actual function and name of the display pieces.

4. Participants are given one point for each correct guess.

DETAILS, DETAILS, DETAILS!

2-4 • Pairs • Observation/Recall • Mild Activity • Short

Object

To observe and recall 10 details about a partner.

How to Play

1. Players face their partners and observe them carefully for one minute.

2. Players then turn their backs to one another and take turns trying to recount 10 details about the other person. Details can range from hair and eye color to number of freckles and jewels.

3. After both partners have had the opportunity to observe one another, players can change partners and try again.

CHALKBOARD MAZES

1-4 • Two or More • Drawing Skills/Creativity/Spatial Abilities • Active • Medium

Materials
chalkboard and colored chalk

Get Started

Draw a maze on the chalkboard. Have each child bring in a magnetic character or create one by gluing a magnet to the back of a tagboard figure, pom-pom character or a figure cut out of a magazine.

Object

To maneuver a magnetic character through the maze.

To create a maze of your own for other players to find their way through.

How to Play

1. After children have seen and maneuvered through your maze, allow one child each day to create a maze.

2. Children who have completed their work and have some spare time or children who select this activity during a choice period may maneuver a magnetic figure through the maze.

CRACK THE CODE

2-4 • Two or More • Pattern Recognition/Problem Solving/Substitution • Sedentary

Get Started

Choose one player to create a code.

Object

To "crack the code" and reveal the secret message.

MUXODY BTODE

How to Play

1. The chosen player presents a coded message for the others on the chalkboard, overhead projector or on paper.

2. The other players attempt to crack the code and discover the secret message.

3. The player who manages to decipher the message is allowed to create their own code and present the next encoded message.

Some Codes to Try

There are many ways to encode a message. Here are some methods you that are appropriate for this age group.

- Number the letters of the alphabet, *A* being *1* and *Z* becoming *26*. Write your message in numbers.

- Scramble each word in the sentence.

- Use backward writing (and provide a mirror)!

- Place a particular letter between every letter of the message.

- Run all the words in the sentences together.

- Write words containing only the letters *A, B, C, D, E, F, G* and encode the letters as notes on a musical staff.

- Substitution Codes. Provide a key where each letter is represented by a particular symbol. In your message replace each letter with its corresponding symbol. Advanced students may be able to solve the message without receiving the key.

92

BABY FACE

K-4 • Group • Recognition/Matching • Mild Activity • Medium

Get Started

Have each child bring in a current and baby photo of themselves. Place the pictures on the chalkboard using Blutak™. Place the current pictures on one side and the baby pictures on another. Number the pictures on both sides.

Object

To match the baby picture with the current picture.

How to Play

1. Have participants draw chalk lines to connect the pictures they think match or record their matches on paper by using the numbers assigned to each picture.

2. The exercise can be "just for fun" or players can compete to see who matches the most pairs correctly.

Variation

• Follow up by attaching string or yarn from each baby picture to the corresponding child picture. It makes a lovely visual for Getting to Know Me, Special Me or graduation themes.

ODOR DETECTIVE

Studying mysteries? Detective stories? The senses? This game will fit right in!

K-4 • Group • Sensory Discrimination • Active • Medium-Long • Cooperative

Materials

things with strong odors: garlic, onions, pine needles, perfume, licorice, bananas, oranges, cloves, coffee, chocolate and so on
cheesecloth
elastic bands
clothespins
string
pencil and paper for each participant

Caution

Ensure that materials used are safe for sniffing. Avoid the use of pepper or chemicals.

Get Started

Wrap items in cheesecloth and secure with elastic bands. Stretch a string between two points in the room at a level slightly above the noses of most members of your group. Using the clothespins, hang the cheesecloth packages from the string. Allow enough space between the packages to keep the odors distinct.

How to Play

1. Explain to the "sniffers" that they may only sniff the packages. Players will lose points for touching.

2. Players will sniff and then record what they think is in each package.

3. When all players have had a chance to "sniff and record" the contents of each packet, the contents can be revealed.

4. Smell Detectives give themselves one point for each correct guess–the player with the most correct sniff guesses is declared the "Grand Nose," "Hound Dog" or "Chief Detective."

WHO'S UNDERCOVER?

K-2 • Group • Critical Analysis/Recall • Active • Short-Medium

Materials
large blanket

Get Started

Select one "detective" to leave the room. Select another child to go "undercover" and hide beneath the blanket.

Object

Detective attempts to guess who is undercover.

How to Play

1. When the detective is out of the room, one player is selected to go undercover.

2. The other players rearrange themselves to throw the detective off the trail.

3. The detective is called back into the room and has three guesses to determine the identity of the "undercover" player.

Variation

• As a follow-up, have successful detectives share their secrets of success. What reasoning skills and methods are effective in this game?

LINE UP RACE

A great exercise in group dynamics and cooperation with skill reinforcement along the way!

1-4 • Group • Group Dynamics/Sequencing • Active • Medium • Cooperative

Materials

timing device

Get Started

Determine an attribute that will be used to organize children in the line up.
Consider age, height, birthdays, alphabetical order of names, shoe size, length of name, hair length . . .

How to Play

1. Announce the attribute players are to line up in accordance with and start the clock.

2. When time is up, all participants must freeze. The leader will check for accuracy of the line up.

Variation

- Discuss the techniques used to accomplish the task. What helped? What didn't? How did the children feel about the actions of others? What skills make a good leader? Why are leaders sometimes needed?

MATCH

A game of matching attributes that develops discriminating thought processes and communication skills.

K-4 • Five or Less Per Group • Matching • Mild Activity • Medium

Get Started

Choose one player to be the "eyeglasses" for the other players. Blindfold the remaining players.

Object

Blindfolded players attempt to end up with a matching pair of blocks.

How to Play

1. The "eyeglasses" player gives each player two of the blocks.

2. In turn the players may ask the "eyeglasses" a question that requires a "yes" or "no" answer.

3. Players will benefit from hearing the questions and answers of others and may ask for another player's block when it is their turn.

4. When it is a player's turn, he may ask another player for her block and then ask one question about the block.

5. The "eyeglasses" will announce a match when one is made and the player who matched the blocks may remove their blindfold.

6 The game ends when each player has a matching pair.

Variation

- Play the game with marbles, geometric shapes, dominoes, golf balls, balloons or stones.

Materials

4 blindfolds for each group
4 pairs of matching blocks (i.e. two dice, two large red blocks, two small red blocks, two small blue blocks)

97

"EYE"DENTIFY

K-4 • Three or More • Visual Discrimination • Mild Activity • Medium

Materials

10 items, i.e. pencil, eraser, shoe, book, apple, bar of soap, skipping rope, etc.
10 hankies or pieces of cloth
paper and pencil for each participant

Get Started

Place 10 items under cloths. Provide each player with paper and a pencil.

Object

To identify the objects under the cloth.

How to Play

1. Have players visually study the items under the cloths. Touching is not allowed.

2. Each player writes down or draws a picture of what they think is under each cloth.

3. When all players have identified 10 items, you can remove the cloths.

4. How many items were children able to guess? Talk about ways that the various items were recognized.

Variation

• For a competitive version of this game, have children check the number of items correctly guessed. The child with the most correct guesses is the winner. Follow up this activity with discussion about shapes of items. What shape is central to the particular pieces? Have the children draw one or all of the items, paying careful attention to the overall shape.

98

TAKE A CLOSE LOOK

2-4 • Two or More • Drawing/Observing Detail • Hands-On • Medium-Long

Materials
pencil and paper

Get Started

Point out small details of various spots in the room. Have children look carefully at their surroundings.

Object

To draw a small section of something in the room.

To identify the subject of other artists' drawings.

How to Play

1. Each player searches the room for an interesting section or small piece of a larger object.

2. The player draws the small section of the object.

3. When all players have completed their drawings, they present them to the class, one at a time. Members of the group attempt to determine the subject of the drawing.

MAPMAKERS

Young mapmakers can learn about world geography through a game.

4 • Group • Social Studies • Hands-On • Medium-Long • Cooperative

Materials

chalkboard and
  chalk
map outlines for
  relevant areas
timing device
bell or whistle

Get Started

Prepare map outlines for relevant areas. These can be traced onto the board, photocopied in sections and taped to the board or projected from an acetate film and overhead projector. Blanks are drawn where players are expected to label continents, countries, states or provinces or towns.

Object

To correctly label the map before the allotted time runs out.

How to Play

1. In turn, have children come up to the board to label a section of the map.

2. The game continues in this manner until all players have provided one label or used their turn to change a label they think is incorrect.

3. When every player has taken one turn, players may elect to "pass," change a label or provide a label for one of the more difficult remaining areas. When the entire map has been labeled correctly, the leader will ring a bell. If all areas have been labeled and the bell has not rung, players will know that the map contains some incorrect labels.

4. Labeling continues until the bell has sounded or the time buzzer has rung.

Variation

- For a competitive version of this game, the group can be divided into two teams and have two map outlines provided. The teams compete against one another to complete their map correctly.

100

PAPER CREATIONS

A simple piece of paper can be folded in many ways for hours of entertaining fun. Paper folding projects provide opportunities for the development of listening skills, following instructions, fine motor skills, creativity and sometimes patience!

Get Started

Provide the group with paper and instructions (verbal or otherwise) for creating the particular paper project.

Materials
scissors
paper
ruler

Object

To turn a piece of paper into a means of fun.

AIRPLANE

A paper airplane is easily made and provides the opportunity for children to experiment with basic principles of aerodynamics. Plan an Air Show to show off the flyers.

How to Make It

1. Fold a rectangular piece of paper vertically in half and then open to make it flat again.
2. Fold the top corners down to meet the center fold line and form small triangles at the top of your page.
3. Fold the top corners down again to meet the center fold and crease well.
4. Fold the plane up in half, recreasing on the center fold, and flatten well.
5. About 2" (5 cm) from the point fold a small portion of the wing down.
6. Flip the plane over and fold the other wing as above.
7. Hold the plane with the center fold at the bottom and fold the tips of the wings back out.
8. Your plane is ready to fly!

How to Play

1. Establish take-off and landing sites. Children throw planes from take-off (taped line on floor) point toward landing area.

    Measure and record distances.

    Add distances of second and third tries.

2. Suspend a plastic hoop or other target from ceiling. Flyers must send their planes through the obstacle.

THE SECRET LETTER

This secret fold and hide letter just might get children writing letters they never knew they could!

1-4 • One • Fine Motor/Language/Following Instructions • Active • Cooperative

Get Started

Write a secret letter on the paper.

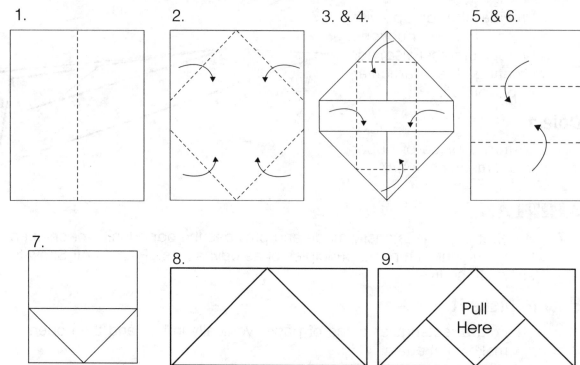

How to Make It

1. Fold the paper in half vertically and then open out again.

2. Fold the four corners into triangles. Bring the points to the center fold line. There will be space left in the center of the page.

3. Fold the two flat edges to meet in the center.

4. Fold the two triangular points towards the center. You will have a rectangular shape.

5. Flip the rectangular shape over so the flat surface is on top.

6. Fold the ends up so the rectangle is folded into thirds then unfold and flatten the rectangle.

7. Fold the bottom third over the middle third.

8. Fold the top third over the previous third and tuck the corners of the top sections into the triangular pockets.

9. Print *Pull Here* on the protruding triangular point.

10. Give the letter to a secret friend!

FORTUNE TELLER

A popular, easy-to-make game, which provides opportunities for counting, reading, writing, using fine motor skills, following instructions and creating fortunes!

1-4 • One • Fine Motor/Language/Following Instructions • Active • Cooperative

How to Make It

1. Fold the paper diagonally in half both ways and mark the center point with a dot.

2. Fold the corners in towards the center so the points meet at the center dot.

3. Flip the small square over and fold the corners to the center once again.

4. Fold this square in half one way, open it and then do so the other way.

5. Gently pull the center point down and push your thumb and forefingers into the four pockets on the sides.

6. Remove your fingers and turn the square over. Print one word on each corner square. These four words might be colors, sports, flowers, music groups, bugs or any other group of words that offer children choice.

7. Flip the square over again and print one numeral on each small triangle. Smaller numbers make the game go faster.

8. Fold the triangles out and print a fortune on each folded half. These fortunes might contain trivia or nonsense.

9. Fold the fortune corners back down to hide the secrets within.

10. Place fingers and thumbs back into the paper pockets and prepare to tell fortunes!

11. First ask participants to make one of the four visible selections. When they do, spell the word they chose flipping the pockets in and out as you do so.

12. After the spelling, the participant chooses one of the numbers that is visible. Flip fingers back and forth again, and stop when the counting is complete.

13. At this point the participant selects one of the numbers and the fortune provided for that number is read.

1 square piece of paper
pencil, pen, marker or crayon

Materials

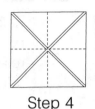

Step 2

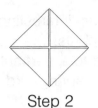

Step 2

Step 4

Step 5

Step 5

BLUE	GREEN
RED	YELLOW

Step 6

Step 7

Step 8

IN FULL VIEW

K-2 • One or More • Observation/Visual Discrimination • Sedentary • Short-Medium

Get Started

Select an interesting object to be hidden. Depending upon the age of the participants, the object can be large or small. Consider using an item related to a particular theme: an autumn leaf, a pretend snowball, a figurine, a spring bird and so on. Choose one "trickster" to hide the object.

How to Play

1. Hold the selected object up for all to see and then have children hide their eyes while the object is hidden.

2. Hide the object in a spot that is visible to all.

3. Instruct players to open their eyes and look for the object.

4. When players spot the object, they raise their hands.

5. When all hands have been raised, or an allotted amount of time has elapsed, one player is selected to retrieve the object.

6. Participants then hide their eyes and the the player who retrieved the object hides it again.

Variation

• Hide the object every day before students arrive at school. When students arrive they may sit down at their seats only when they have sighted the object. This is a good way to get students into the classroom, seated and ready to begin the day!

104

FOLLOW THE CLAPPING CLUES

K-2 • Group • Auditory Discrimination/Estimation • Active • Short • Cooperative

Materials
none

Get Started

Select one player to be IT.

How to Play

1. IT leaves the room and another player selects the "secret object" in the room–a player's shoes, a particular book, desk, window, the clock, etc. All members of the group are shown the object.

2. IT returns to the group and slowly moves around the room. The class attempts to direct IT to the object with clapping clues. When IT is close to the object, the class claps loudly. When IT is far from the object, the class claps very lightly. When IT is very far from the object, the group stops clapping.

3. When the object is discovered, IT may choose another IT and the game continues for another round.

HIDE THE THIMBLE

An old favorite that keeps the seeker, the hider and the audience engaged!
K-2 • Group • Estimation • Mild Activity • Short

Materials
1 thimble

Get Started

Choose one student to be the "seeker" and send her out into the hall. Choose another child to hide the thimble.

Object

Seeker: To find the thimble.

Others: To help the seeker find the thimble.

How to Play

1. The thimble is hidden and the seeker returns to the classroom.

2. The seeker moves around the classroom while the group directs him to the thimble with calls of "You're getting hot, cold, hotter; you're burning up; you're freezing" and so on until the seeker finds the thimble.

PENCIL GAMES FOR LEARNING AND FUN

Pencil and paper has been used for learning and games as long as it has been around. It provides an easy way to keep all children involved and busy as they learn. There are many old favorite pencil and paper games to challenge one's creativity, problem-solving abilities and strategic skills.

DOTS AND BOXES

A simple game of strategy and fun!

1-4 • Two • Strategy/Concentration • Sedentary • Short-Long

Get Started

Draw rows of dots in a square formation. Ten dots long and 10 dots wide makes a good start. You might want to start small or, if you have all day, you might want to make rows and rows and rows!

How to Play

1. The first player draws a line between two dots.

2. The second player draws a line between any two dots and so on.

3. Players attempt to be the one to add the fourth line that closes a box. When a player closes a box, he claims the box by putting his initials in it. He is then allowed to add one more line–which often leads to another box and another line and so on.

4. Players take turns drawing lines until all of the dots have been connected and all of the squares have been claimed.

5. When the game is over, players count the number of boxes they have claimed. The player who has claimed the most boxes wins.

Variation

• Fill a large portion of the chalkboard with rows of dots before children come to school or a party. Divide the group into two teams. Throughout the day or the get-together, players who have completed tasks can join the ongoing Dots and Boxes game putting the team initials in a box whenever a box is claimed. Play may continue only when at least one player from each team is present. When more than one player is present for a particular team, then the members will take turns drawing a line. At the end of the day, week or party, the giant Dots and Boxes game will be tallied and a winning team will be announced.

TIC-TAC-TOE

A simple game of logic and fun that can keep minds active during short transition times.

K-4 • Two • Strategy/Concentration • Sedentary • Short

Get Started

Draw the gameboard. Establish which player will go first. This player chooses whether to play Xs or Os.

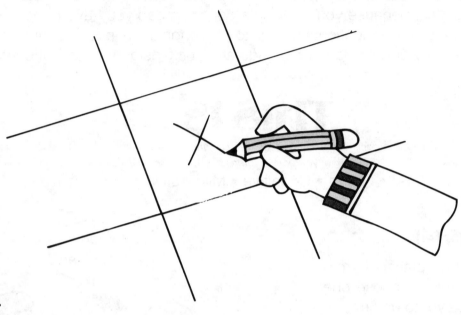

Object

To complete a line consisting of your figure (X or O) before your opponent does.

How to Play

1. The first player places her mark in one of the nine spaces on the game grid.

2. The second player places the X or O in one of the spaces and so on until one player gets three in a row and calls "Three in a row! Tic-Tac-Toe!"

3. If all spaces are filled and neither player has completed a line, the game is declared a Cat's Game and no one wins the round. If all spaces are filled and neither player has completed a line, the game is declared a Cat's Game and no one wins the round.

Variation

• This game can be played on a permanent Xs and Os surface taped on the floor, painted on the chalkboard or made out of wood. The markers can be made with removable markers, chalk, magnetic figures, marbles, live players or other figures to correspond with a book or theme being studied in class.

107

ACTION GAMES FOR INDOOR FUN

Sitting around indoors can put a mind and body asleep, especially if you're a kid. Take a fresh approach to your indoor time and help keep kids keen and alert to process information and new skills. Just because you are inside doesn't mean you have to be inactive. This chapter offers active, educational games to challenge the mind, body and spirit–especially on those rainy or cold days when kids are stuck inside with lots of energy to burn.

THIS IS . . .

This wacky little game fills in time with challenging, thought-provoking fun! What you say and what you point to aren't always the same thing.

1-4 • Group • Cognitive • Mild Active • Cooperative

Materials

Get Started

Have players form a circle. Choose one player to go first.

Object

To touch the body part stated by the previous player while calling it another.

This is my knee.

How to Play

1. The leading player touches one body part stating that it is another body part. For example, This is my . . . says "nose" but touches head.

2. The next player touches his nose but calls it something else. For example, "This is my arm" (but touches the body part stated by the previous player, in this example the nose).

3. The fun proceeds in this manner around the circle until all players have had an opportunity to touch and speak and get mixed up!

INDOOR SCAVENGER HUNTS

Combine the fun of a hunt with the learning or reinforcement of new skills.

PreK-4 • Group • Communication/Problem Solving • Active • Long

Get Started

Prepare a list or topic of items to be hunted for.

How to Play

1. Provide participants with a list of items to be hunted for. These items can be recorded or checked off on the list as necessary.

2. Allow students to scavenge around the room, house or school to find the particular items.

3. When all participants have completed the hunt, you can review their findings and provide solutions to any objects not found. If you are hosting a competitive contest, you can check the findings and declare the player who found the most items the winner.

Consider the following hunts:

NUMBER HUNT

Find the numbers 1 to 20 around the school. Record the place where each number was discovered.

LETTER HUNT

Find the letter ____ around the school.

WORD HUNT

Find words that start with the letter _____.

PARENT AND CHILD SCAVENGER HUNT

Familiarize parents and new students with the school. Prepare a scavenger list for kindergarten introduction to school, open house or a class party. Take this opportunity to have students show parents around the classroom and school. Ask other staff members if they may be included as objects of the hunt–it's a great opportunity for parents to meet the principal, librarian, secretaries, special education teachers and so on. If there is a parent resource library, room or PTA information center, be sure to include it, too.

THE ALPHABET
SCAVENGER HUNT

Find one object for each letter of the alphabet and draw a picture of it in the following rectangles.

Aa

Jj

Ss

Bb

Kk

Tt

Cc

Ll

Uu

Dd

Mm

Vv

Ee

Nn

Ww

Ff

Oo

Xx

Gg

Pp

Yy

Hh

Qq

Zz

Ii

Rr

RIGHT SHOE, LEFT SHOE

K-3 • Pairs • Right/Left Recognition/Putting on Shoes • Medium

Get Started

Players sit in a straight line or in a circle formation.

How to Play

1. The first player stomps her left foot and then her right. The player to her right stomps his left foot and then right and so on around the circle to keep the rhythm for this little rhyme:

   Right shoe, left shoe

   Change your own shoes!

   (One word is chanted with each foot stomp.)

2. The player whose foot stomps as the verse ends must change her shoes to the wrong feet. If the rhyme stops at this player again, her shoes will then be changed back to the right feet.

3. Play continues in this manner until the music is stopped by the leader or until the allotted time runs out. Players who have their shoes on the right feet are the winners, players who do not can't change their luck but can change their shoes back!

Note

This game can help younger children learn to put shoes on and off.

Lacing is optional!

Variation

- This game will work well for an outdoor sandal party or an indoor (dry) rubber boot party.

WHO HAS THE BEANBAG?

K-2 • Group • Guessing • Mild Active • Medium

Materials
beanbag

Get Started

Choose one player to sit in the middle of the circle. The other players form a tightly packed circle around this player.

How to Play

1. Have the player in the middle close his eyes.

2. Other players pass a beanbag behind their backs and count aloud from 1 to 10.

3. On the count of 10, the beanbag is held, and the player in the middle can open her eyes.

4. The player in the center has two opportunities to guess who has the beanbag. If she guesses correctly, she may take another turn in the middle. If she does not guess correctly, she must trade places with player holding the beanbag.

GUESS THE GREETER

1-4 • Group • Auditory Discrimination Recall • Sedentary • Short

Materials
none

Get Started

Choose one player to be IT.

Object

Greeter: To make his voice unrecognizable.

IT: To try to determine the identity of the greeter after hearing his voice.

Good morning!

How to Play

1. IT faces the wall in a corner.

2. The leader chooses another child to greet IT with "Good morning, _____."

3. IT then faces the group and tries to identify the greeter.

4. If IT guesses correctly, using two chances, she may take another turn. If she does not guess the identity, then the greeter becomes IT.

TIME OUT

*If your imagination is a little dim and you can't think of a game to refresh
your group, try a little music and movement.*

K-4 • Any Number • Exercise • Active • Cooperative • Transition

Get Started

Have children stand. Start the music.

How to Play

1. When the music starts, lead the group in some simple head-to-toe stretches.

2. As participants become comfortable with moving to the music, they can lead stretches and exercises or turn the musical calisthenics into a jiving hip-hop of free flow rejuvenation!

3. Take these refreshed minds and bodies onto the next learning task!

THE IROQUOIS PEACH STONE GAME

K-4 • Two or More • Multiculturalism • Counting/Coordination • Active Short-Medium

Materials

stones, peach stones or almonds in the shell

wooden or plastic bowl

pebbles or tokens of some sort

black felt tip markers or black paint

Get Started

Paint or color one side of each stone or nut. Put the stones in the bowl. Decide which player or team will go first.

How to Play

1. The first player, or team member, tosses the stones up and catches them in the bowl. She then counts how many stones landed black side up and collects that many pebbles or tokens.

2. The next player, or member of the opposing team, tosses the stones and collects points in the same manner.

3. Play continues until each player has had one turn or until every team member has had a turn.

4. The player or team with the most points at the end of the game wins.

The Iroquois people traditionally played this game during the eighth and final day of their mid-winter festival. The game indicated that the world was as the Creator intended it to be. The traditional game uses two teams and 100 peach stones burned black on one side.

CHARADES

A popular game for all ages!

K-4 • Four or More • Drama/Communication • Active • Medium-Long

Materials

timer
hat
slips of paper
box (optional)

Get Started

Choose book titles, phrases, songs, animals and characters from recently studied books to print on slips of paper. These can be submitted by students and then screened for appropriateness or prepared by the teacher or game leader. Place the slips in a box. Break the group into at least two teams of two to six players.

How to Play

1. Set the timer for one to three minutes.

2. The first team chooses a player to pick a slip of paper and act out the item without speaking. The player's team attempts to guess the item. If the team guesses the item in the allotted time, they get a point. If time runs out, they do not. In either case, play passes to the next team.

3. The next team picks a slip and plays the game in the same way and so on until every player has had the opportunity to act out an item.

CHARADE LINGO

Introduce players to the various actions used in a game of charades.

To indicate:

We're starting	Spread palms, facedown
A play	Bow or curtsey
A book	Clasp hands together and open them to resemble a book cover
Film	Cupped hand for a movie camera and wind the other hand
Song	Impression of an opera singer
TV program	Draw a box in the air
The number of words in the title	Hold up one finger for each word
Whole item will be conveyed at once	Draw a large encompassing circle in the air
Mime each word separately	Hold up the number of fingers to show the position of the word in the item
Constituent syllables	Hold up fingers to indicate the number of syllables and tap them on the forearm
Particular syllable	Tap the number of fingers to show the position of the syllable in the word
A/An	Rounding the index finger and thumb
The	T shape using the index fingers
Sounds like	Pull on ear
Guessed it!	Touch index finger to end of nose.

WHAT AM I?

A simple variation of charades without the technical details.

K-4 • Two or More • Communication/Information Recall • Active • Medium-Long

Get Started

Decide if you are going to act out animals, machines, community helpers, professions or any other theme-related object that works! Choose one player to go first.

How to Play

1. The first player acts out the chosen item and the others try to guess what the player is.

2. The player who guesses correctly becomes the player who acts out in the next round of the game.

LAUGH MASTER

This game is sure to lighten the mood!

K-4 • Group • Fun/Drama • Active • Short

Get Started

Appoint one player as the Laugh Master.

How to Play

1. Laugh Master attempts to make the other children laugh or talk.

2. A child who is made to laugh or talk joins the Laugh Master.

3. The game continues until all players have become the Laugh Master.

Try This

• You may need to set a time and/or noise limit for this game.

• Determine ahead of time a title for a player who cannot be made to laugh.

MIRROR PANTOMIME

1-4 • Pairs • Body Awareness/Dramatic Expression • Active • Cooperative
Short-Medium

Get Started

Have players select partners or pair them in appropriate pairs.

Object

To mirror the movements of your partner.

How to Play

1. Have players face their partners.
2. One player is chosen to lead first, and the other acts as the mirror reflection.
3. The leader moves face and body, slowly, in any way possible. The "reflection" attempts to follow. It is best to start it with slow, easy movements.
4. The players reverse roles.

Variations

- Lead into this activity by having children use a real mirror to observe their reflections in a new way.
- Provide music for movements as children become more proficient at this activity.
- Prepare presentations using this technique.

THUMB CHALLENGE

This game gets a thumbs up for excitement and challenge.

2-4 • Pairs • Sportsmanship/Manual Dexterity • Hand Action • Short • Transition

Get Started

Have players form pairs.

Object

To pin your opponent's thumb under your own and avoid having your own thumb wrestled down.

How to Play

1. Players join their curled fingers with their opponents' opposite hand (right hands with left hands) and they keep their thumbs sticking up as shown.

2. Players repeat together

One, two, three, four	*thumbs move back and forth*
I declare a thumb war.	*thumb straight up*
Kiss	*thumbs touch*
Hug	*thumbs touch side by side*
And begin!	*thumbs try to pin the other down*

3. The player who pins the other player's thumb down wins the round. Players usually play the best two out of three.

4. Winners take on winners and losers challenge losers for an informal round robin to find the "thumb champion."

DREIDEL FUN

A traditional game of the Hanukkah celebrations using a four-sided spinning top called a dreidel.

1-4 • Two to Four • Multiculturalism/Recognizing Symbols • Hands-On • Medium

Materials

2" (5 cm) square piece of tag-board
brass fastener
arrow cut from 1¹/₂" x ¹/₄" (4 x 1.25 cm) tag-board
marker
gelt (foil-wrapped chocolate coins given as gifts during Hanukkah) or pennies

On a traditional dreidel the Hebrew words are shown as Hebrew letters. The letters are the initials of the Hebrew words meaning "a great miracle happened here." These refer to the story of the miracle of the oil in the temple lamp.

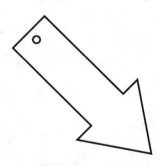

Get Started

MAKE THE DREIDEL SPINNER

1. On the square piece of tag-board, draw a diagonal line from one corner of the square to the opposing corner and then from the remaining corner to the other to divide the square into four equal sections.

2. Write one of the four Hebrew words in each section:

   Nun, meaning "none"

   Gimmel, meaning "all"

   Hey, meaning "half"

   Shin, meaning "spin again"

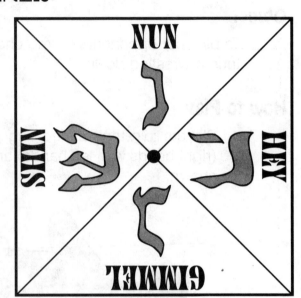

3. Poke a hole where the lines intersect on the tagboard. Poke the brass fastener through the arrow and attach to the spinner.

4. Divide the coins among the players.

   If using pennies, drop them in a solution of vinegar and baking soda to shine them so they may better represent the "gelt."

How to Play

1. Each player places two coins in the pot before the game begins.

2. The first player spins the dreidel and acts according to the word that is shown.

   Nun: The player takes nothing from the pot and play passes to the next player.

   Gimmel: The player takes all of the tokens and each player puts two back into the pot for the next round.

   Hey: The player takes half of the coins in the pot.

   Shin: The player may spin again.

3. Play continues in this manner until one player has won all of the "gelt" in the pot.

SHADOW MAKERS

K-4 • One • Chalkboard • Active • Short

Get Started

Hang a large sheet in front of the chalkboard, or use a film screen or white wall. Focus the light onto the white area, leaving a space between the board and the light for children to stand and make hand shapes.

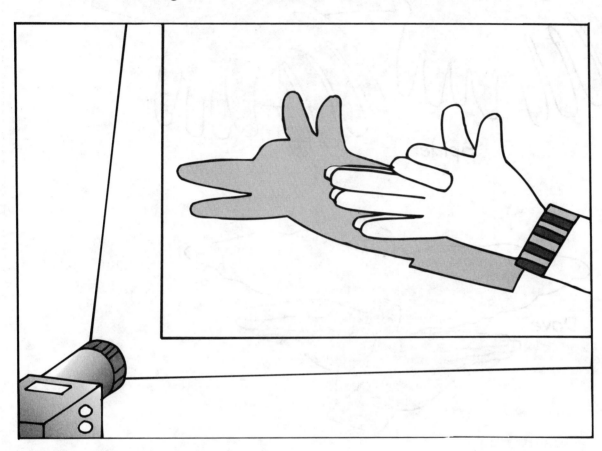

Object

To explore shadow shapes.

How to Play

1. The shadow maker stands in front of the light source, between the light and the white surface.

2. She uses her creativity, spatial abilities and hands to create shapes, letters, insects, creatures and more.

Variation

- Extend the activity with shadow plays, character creations, tracings of the shapes or creative poems or stories about the shadow characters.

SHADOW CHARACTERS

Try the following shadow creations:

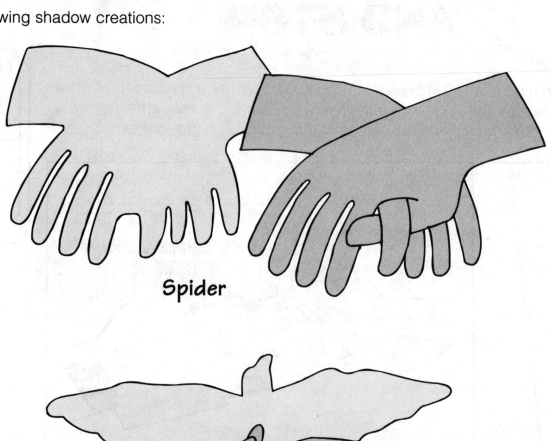

Spider

Dove

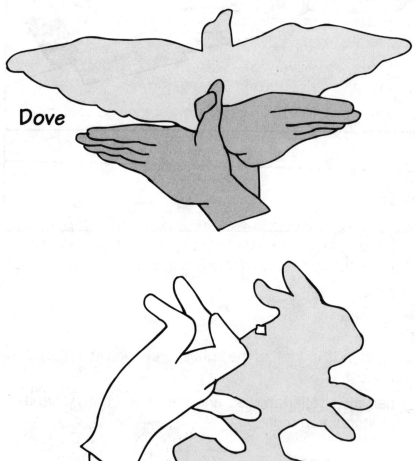

Rabbit

MOVE TO THE MUSIC AND STOP

A good transition activity to break up sedentary activities

K-1 • Group • Movement/Music • Active • Short Transition Game

Get Started

Instruct students to move with the music and freeze when it stops. Select one player to stop and start the music (or do this yourself). Choose one player to catch students who don't move when the music is playing or move when it has stopped.

Object

To "freeze" when the music stops.

How to Play

1. Students stand and spread out around the indoor space.

2. When the music starts, participants move to the rhythm. Players not moving are asked to sit down.

3. When the music stops, all players must freeze. The leader may ask those who move after the music stops to be seated.

4. The game continues until only one player is left moving and freezing–and the rest of the group is refreshed and sitting ready for the next activity.

ALL IN TOGETHER

The leader can "catch" players who move after the music has stopped by calling their name, but all players remain in the game in this just-for-fun version that allows all participants to stay in the game until everyone has had enough!

LIKES ATTRACT

Players move to the music, but when it stops they are instructed to form groups with players who:

> have names that start with the same letter
>
> have the same number of siblings
>
> have the same favorite color
>
> are the same age
>
> have the same birthday month
>
> and so on . . .

SQUARE DANCE

Get things hopping and swirling with an old-time square dance.
It won't take long for boys and girls to discover the fun and fast action of this indoor activity.

2-4 • Eight • Music/Coordination/Fitness • Active • Medium-Long

Materials

large open dance
space
recorded music or
live fiddler
(optional)

---

*Many square
dance tunes can
be found on the
old 45 rpms or
78 rpms. Look
for these old
favorites:*

*Maple Sugar by
by Ned Landry*

*Road to the Isles
by Harry Hibbs*

*Hannigan's
Hornpipe by
Don Messer
and His
Islanders*

*The Rocket Reel
by King Ganam*

Get Started

If possible, watch a group of experienced square dancers in action. Begin learning without the use of music. Have the eight participants form pairs and become couples 1, 2, 3 and 4. The girls stand at the right of their partners. Have the couples form a square as shown on page 126. This is called the set.

How to Square Dance

Familiarize students with the terms and associated actions one at a time. Have them practice each move until it comes easily and smoothly. Review the old steps whenever you learn a new one and practice them altogether with music. Introduce participants to the following terms and steps:

Form up four couples to a set: The couples form a set as shown on page 126.

Stand and clap: Players stand in formation and clap in time to the music.

Allemande left to the corners all: The four ladies face to their right and the gents face to their left.

The ladies and gents then link their right elbows and turn around twice.

Practice this several times and then try the clap and allemande left to the music with someone calling the actions.

Right hand to your partner and grand chain all: The gents move clockwise right and then left around the set, and shaking the right and then left hand of the person they meet.

The ladies move counterclockwise in the same manner around the set.

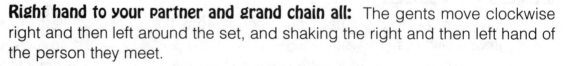

Swing: The boy puts his right hand on the girl's waist and takes her left hand in his left hand.

The girl puts her right hand on the boy's left shoulder and her left hand in his.

The couple places their feet in a position that allows them to "swing" around and around in a clockwise circle while maintaining their footing position.

Swing when you meet: Have dancers give their right hand to their partner and all grand chain until they meet their partner in the set. When the partners meet, they swing together.

First couple turn to the right, Lady in the center and three go round: The couple in the first position turns to the second couple. The girl stands in the middle, and the boy joins hands with this couple.

The three swing around the girl in the middle three times.

Lady fly out and the gent fly in: The center girl joins the other couple, and the boy goes into the center while the three swing around three times.

The other couples clap to the music and watch the fun.

Now swing in the middle and six go round: The first couple moves into the center of the set.

The other couples join hands and turn around the center couple.

First couple to the third: The first couple then moves to the third couple and repeats the procedure above with the third couple and then moves to the center and then on to the fourth couple.

First couple to the fourth: Couples carry on as above.

When the first couple returns back to their original position, they Allemande left grand chain and swing (see above).

Now, second to the third: The second couple goes to the third and repeats the process completed by the first couple as above.

Now, third to the fourth: Repeat the process.

And fourth to the first: Repeat the process.

Do-Se-Do: Partners face one another and take a step forward on the right foot, passing right shoulders. Then step to the side with the right foot, passing back to back. Then step backwards with the right foot, passing left shoulders. Step to the side with the left foot, passing face-to-face and return to original position.

THE DANCE CALL

Form four couples to a set.
Are you ready?

Now allemande left to the corners all
Right hand to partner and grand chain all
Your left foot up and your right foot down
Hurry up there–you will never get around
Swing when you meet.

First couple turn to the right
Lady in the center and three go round
Lady fly out and the gent fly in–three go round
Now swing in the middle and six go round
First couple turn to the third
Lady in center and three go round
Lady fly out and gent fly in–three go round
Swing in the middle and six go round.
First couple to the fourth
Lady in center and three go round
Lady fly out and gent fly in–three
  go round
Swing in the middle and six go
  round.

And so on . . . second couple . . .
  third couple . . . and fourth
  couple to the . . .

Back to your partners, do-se-do!
Gents, salute your ladies and
  ladies curtsy low!

First Couple

Second Couple

Fourth Couple

Third Couple

Variations

- Invite some experienced dancers to help your group get off to a good start.

- Practice and prepare a dance performance for the school concert or a Parents' Day in the school.

- Talk about the names of tunes like "The Crooked Stove Pipe," "The Irish Washerwoman" and "Apple Blossom Hoe-Down." Where did these tunes come from?

- When were these dances popular? Have children make up song titles of their own.

126

COOPERATIVE MUSICAL CHAIRS

A sometimes rowdy, indoor game of quick action and fun.

K-2 • Six or More • Quick Action/Cooperation • Active • Cooperative • Medium

Materials

chairs
music

Get Started

Select one music "director." Place the chairs back to back in an open space.

How to Play

1. The music director starts the music and players move around the chairs to the music.

2. The director stops the music and players attempt to find a chair. For the first round there are enough chairs for all players.

3. Now, one chair is removed and the music starts again. When the music stops, players find a chair as before, however, one chair is missing so players must find a way to accommodate each player. Giggling, cooperating and sharing of chairs is allowed.

Variation

- Try this game using hoops instead of chairs. Place the hoops around the room and remove one a time. It is great fun trying to fit the whole group into one hoop!

TOUCH WOOD AND WHISTLE

An active indoor game with a no running rule that keeps the game safe and challenging!

1-4 • Group • Following Rules/Recognition of Wood Products/Whistling • Active Medium

Materials

safe open play area
objects made of wood

Get Started

Select one player to be IT. Establish a NO running rule.

Object

IT: To tag another player.

Players: To avoid being tagged by IT.

How to Play

1. IT faces a wall and counts to five. Other players move away from IT while he counts.

2. On the count of "five," IT moves around the room in an attempt to tag other players. A player who runs in this tag game is required to sit out for one minute.

3. A player is deemed "safe" when they touch anything made of wood and whistle, but one's whistle can only last so long!

4. When a player is tagged, she becomes IT and the game continues.

5. The game ends when time is called.

INDOOR HOPSCOTCH MATH

K-4 • One or More • Gross Motor/Math • Active • Medium

Materials
flat surface
masking tape or
   chalk
1 marker per
   player

Get Started

Using masking tape or chalk, mark a hopscotch grid on the classroom floor. Your grid can be of any shape, size or style. Number each box or segment of your hopscotch grid.

Object

To be the first player to journey through the hopscotch grid, adding and/or subtracting correctly as you go.

How to Play

1. In turn, players attempt to hop through the board in typical hopscotch fashion: on one foot, except on side-by-side squares where one foot is permitted in each box at the same time. Hop the board without stepping on lines or putting two feet in a single box. When the player reaches the last box, he must turn around in one jump and repeat the one- and two-foot hopping and jumping sequence back and out of the board.

2. When a player has successfully completed the hopping sequence there and back through the board, he may try the math version of the game. On the journey through the board the player must add the numbers aloud as he lands in each box. For example, the first box is marked 0 and the second marked 1, the third marked 2. The player will announce "0" and then "1" and then "3" and so on until all of the numbers have been added on the way up the board and on the way back. By the time a player reaches the end of the game he will announce the sum of all of the numbers added on the way there and back and will have successfully completed the game. A player who steps on a line, puts two feet in a single box or miscalculates, will lose their turn and begin again on her next turn.

3. When all members of the group have mastered the math of the particular board, the numbers will be changed to present a new hopping and adding challenge.

Variation

• Players can try adding as they proceed up the board and subtracting as they come back down.

BOUNCE AND COUNT

*Young children can learn to count and older ones to multiply
with the rhythmic bounce motion and the rhythm of the facts.*

K-2 • Any Number • Counting/Math Facts Coordination • Active

Materials

1 ball per child
surface that can
be used to
bounce a ball

Get Started

Provide each child with a ball and a floor or wall and a math task.
Consider having players count by ones, twos, threes and so on, depen-
dent upon their abilities.

How to Play

Set kids up with a ball and let them bounce and count as they exercise
and learn the facts! Encourage one bounce for each number to introduce
rhythm.

Variations

• Have the entire group bounce and count in unison for some rhythm and
  bounce math reinforcement.

• Turn this activity into a presentation for parents.

INDOOR BASKETBALL

A quiet, active, indoor game for students who have spare moments between activities.

1-3 • One or Two • Addition/Ball-Handling Skills • Active • Medium

Get Started

Shape a metal hoop from a coat hanger and fasten it to a wall, door or cupboard using the tape or another suitable method. Find a sponge ball or blow up a balloon that will fit through the hoop. Use masking tape to mark Xs on the floor. Number the Xs closest to the hoop with a lower value than those placed a further distance from the hoop.

Materials

coat hanger
packing tape
balloon or sponge
  ball

Object

To get the ball through the hoop.

How to Play

1. Players take turns attempting to toss the ball through the hoop from various marked spots on the floor. Each player gets five turns and may choose which *X* to throw from. When the ball goes through the hoop, the player collects the number of points marked on the *X* thrown from.

2. Each player tosses five times and then tallies her score.

3. The player with the highest score wins.

Variations

- Provide a scoring chart where players can record their high scores. Other players can attempt to beat the highest class score.

- Try a game of Silent Basketball. Any player who makes a noise during the game will lose a point.

TAKRAW

A variation of a traditional game from Thailand that is sure to liven things up!

K-2 • Group • Multiculturalism • Coordination/Group Dynamics • Active
Cooperative • Medium

Materials

1 balloon (and a spare in case of a blow up)

Get Started

Have the group stand in a circle and hold hands.

Object

To stay in your own space and not let the balloon hit the ground.

How to Play

1. The leader tosses the balloon in the air. Players attempt to keep the balloon from hitting the ground by using any part of their body necessary.

2. The particular round of the game ends when the balloon touches the ground or two players disconnect their hands.

Variations

HANDS FREE VERSION

Younger children can play an easier version of the game where they do not join hands.

BALLOON VOLLEY

For a competitive version of the game, divide the group into two teams. Draw a line or place a rope down the middle of your room. The teams attempt to keep the balloon up when it is on their side of the court but make the balloon hit the ground in the opposing court. When the balloon touches the ground on one side of the court, the team on the other side gains a point.

GET IT THERE SAFELY

1-4 • Group • Coordination • Active • Cooperative • Medium

Get Started

Provide each player with one balloon. Mark starting and finishing lines. Set up a safe obstacle course.

Object

To have the entire group successfully complete the course before the allotted time runs out.

How to Play

1. Players are set off from the starting line at different times. They must travel to the finish line, keeping their balloon in the air. Each player will count how many times their balloon hits the ground before they reach the finish line.

2. Players continue traveling the track until they have completed the entire course without letting the balloon fall. Players who have completed the course become a cheering section for the other players.

Materials

1 balloon per child
timing device
everyday items to make an obstacle course (broom, chalk, eraser, desks, books, etc.)

Start

Finish

BODY LETTERS

K-1 • One or More • Alphabet Recognition/Body Awareness • Active • Medium

Materials

1 set of alphabet cards (one card for each letter of the alphabet)

hat or other container

Get Started

Familiarize players with the letters of the alphabet. Choose one student to be the leader.

Object

To form letters of the alphabet.

How to Play

1. The leader pulls alphabet cards from the hat and all players attempt to form their bodies into that letter. (You might want to set a time limit.)

2. The leader pulls another alphabet letter from the hat and players change their positions and so on.

Variations

• Have children work in small groups to form the letters.

• Use only upper or lowercase letters.

• If you have an especially large group, you might want to try some two- or three-letter words.

BODY TWIST

K-1 • Two or More • Recognition • Active • Medium

Get Started

Prepare the game playing surface. The vinyl sheet should have four each of four different symbols marked on it. For example, four red circles, four yellow circles, four orange and four blue or four each of various numbers (or math symbols); four each of various shapes, letters or words. Choose one player to spin the spinner and call out the symbols, numbers or colors.

Object

To gain experience listening, recognizing symbols, stretching and twisting the body and having fun!

Materials

vinyl sheet marked with numbers or letters or tape markings on the floor

spinner with corresponding symbols to those on the floor or gameboard

How to Play

1. Players stand, facing the game surface and listen to the caller.

2. The caller spins the spinner and calls out the symbol, number or color indicated.

3. A player places her hand or foot over one of the symbols called. Any player who places a hand or foot off of the symbols or who falls is disqualified from this round of the game.

4. The first player to have two hands and two feet covering the called symbols (without falling!) wins the game and becomes the new caller.

HELP ME UP!

1-4 • Pairs • Problem Solving/Coordination • Active • Short-Medium • Cooperative

Get Started

Have the group choose partners.

Object

To work together to stand up from a back to back, arms linked, sitting position.

How to Play

1. Partners sit on the ground back to back, link their arms at the elbows and bend their knees.
2. The pairs attempt to stand up while remaining back to back with linked arms.

TIED IN KNOTS

2-4 • Group • Cognitive Challenge • Active • Medium • Cooperative

Get Started

Divide players into groups of no more than six. Have each group form a tight circle with players standing shoulder to shoulder.

Object

To work as a group to untangle the knot.

How to Play

1. Players join their right hands with the right hand of any player other than the players on either side of them.
2. Players then join their left hands with players not on either side of them.
3. Now for the challenge! Players attempt to unravel the human knot without disconnecting their hands.

READY, AIM!

A simple, active transition exercise that kids love!

K-4 • Any Number • Hand-Eye Coordination • Transition

Get Started

Instruct players to aim and throw their objects into the pail from wherever they are. Remind children of rules of safety and respect for others if necessary.

How to Play

Players attempt to throw their small objects into the pail. These objects can be collected or left in the pail. Erasers make a good tossing object as they can be imprinted with children's initials and easily identified for an effortless return of items. Items can also be left in the pail. The activity makes a good wrap-up for a pop-quiz that children don't really want to take home! Just crumple those papers and aim!

Materials

empty trash pail or other bucket-like container

small objects, at least one per player

BEANBAG TOSS

An easy game that can be played anywhere-over desks, in hallways, over bookshelves or wherever you find yourself!

1-4 • Pairs • Hand-Eye Coordination • Medium • Transition

How to Play

Players stand one tile length (or foot length, if you have no floor markings) and toss the beanbag from one player to another and back again. If this is completed without the bag being dropped, then the players move back one tile or foot length and try again. If a beanbag is dropped, players must go back to the beginning position and try again.

Materials

1 beanbag per player

Variation

• Players may decide that they will not move back to the start when a bag is missed but remain in the particular spot until they have success. Pairs may compete against other pairs or against the clock.

137

FAN BALL

1-4 • Group • Sportsmanship • Active • Medium

Materials

1 large flat desk-
  top
1 Ping-Pong™ ball
paper fan for
  each player

Get Started

Each player folds a piece of paper in ¼" (.6 cm) strips, accordion-style, to make a paper fan. The group is divided into two teams. The team members are positioned on opposing sides of the table.

Object

To "blow" the ball off of the table on the opponent's side of the table, but keep the ball on the table when it is on your side of the table.

How to Play

1. The ball is dropped in the middle of the table.

2. Players fan the ball so that it crosses the center line into the opponent's side of the table. Players may not cross the center line into the opposing team's space or touch the ball with their fan or any part of their body.

3. If the ball falls off of the table on one team's side, the opposing team gains a point.

138

INDOOR GOLF

A game to challenge the skills of putting and addition!

1-4 • One or More • Addition/Coordination • Active • Medium-Long

Get Started
PREPARE THE GOLF COURSE

Cover the cans or tubes in foil or paper adhered with glue or tape. Nail, screw or hot-glue the cans in a row along the 1" x 2" (2.5 x 5 cm), ensuring that one side of the cans forms a flat edge. Mix the large and small cans in a random pattern. Lay the cans on their sides with the wood at the back.

MAKE YOUR MARKERS

Indicate a scoring point on the craft sticks. Glue the craft sticks to the back of the tins using a hot glue gun. The larger cans should be marked with the lower value numbers.

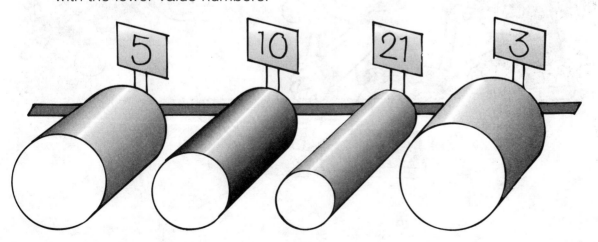

MAKE THE GOLF CLUBS

If you do not have any toy golf clubs, make your own. Attach a sponge to the base of wood doweling using rubber bands. It makes a great putter!

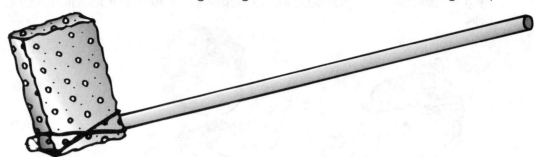

How to Play

1. Players can compete against others or try to better their own score.

2. A player must place their ball behind the putting line and put it into a tin can "hole." She collects the points indicated by the marker on the tin her ball successfully goes into. Play then passes to the next player. If the ball does not go into a hole, it is left in position until the golfer's next turn.

3. Points are added up throughout the game. Each player is allowed five putts. The player with the highest score after each player has taken five putts is declared the winner.

THIS IS A BALL

3-4 • Group • Concentration • Active • Medium

Get Started

Players get into a circle formation.

Object

To pass the object, ask and answer the question without getting mixed up!

How to Play

1. The first player passes an object to the next player and says, "This is a _____."

2. The second player asks, "A what?" and the leader repeats, "A _____." The second player then passes the object to a third player and repeats, "This is a _____." The third player asks, "A what?" passing it back to the second player. The second player then passes back to the leader and asks, "A what?" The leader passes the object back repeating that name of the object. The answer and the object is passed back through the line repeating what it is until the fourth player receives the object and asks, "A what?" and so on. The object must go all the way back to leader each time!

3. Play continues in this manner, with one more player included in the passing of the object in each round until all players are included in the passing line.

Variation

• To complicate things even further and to keep more players active, introduce two objects at the same time–each traveling in a different direction!

INDOOR RACES

Safe activities to get kids moving without the fast pace of an outdoor race.

K-4 • Group • Coordination/Sportsmanship/Motor Development
Active • Short-Medium

Materials

flat, obstacle-free stretch where at least two players can move (between desk rows will work)
start and finish lines
various objects for each student: eraser, ruler, book, broom, etc.

Get Started

Explain the rules of the chosen race, emphasizing indoor safety. Clear a path for racers to travel. Mark a start and finish line with string, chalk or masking tape.

Object

To have fun in a controlled race, balancing various objects and moving.

BALANCING RACES

1. Competitors balance an eraser on the flat end of a ruler and hold it at arm's length in front of them as they wait at the starting line.

2. The leader signals the start of the race with a bell or the simple call of "Ready, set, go!"

3. On the signal, players proceed from the start to the finish line. If the eraser drops enroute, the player must return to the start line and try again. This tends to encourage a slower-paced race!

Variations

- Try the following items for interesting variations of this race:

    a book on a broom

    an egg (or small ball) on a spoon

    a book on one's head

    a playground ball in a baseball mitt

- Use the opposite hand. (Children who are right-handed must use their left and vice versa.)

- "Race" backwards.

- Race with shoes on opposite feet.

WADDLE RACE

Competitors waddle from the start to the finish in a squatting position with their hands on their hips. Any player who falls or touches the ground is sent back to the start line.

Variation

- Try racing like a crab or by placing one foot directly in front of the other.

Good Sport Award

In recognition of _____
for demonstrating outstanding skills of fair play.

Signed: _____

Date: _____

Achievement Award

Awarded to _____
         for outstanding achievement in

_____.

Signed: _____

Date: _____

AWARD OF PARTICIPATION

This award is presented to _____
in recognition of outstanding effort, enthusiasm and
participation in _____
on _____

Signed: _____

Date: _____

BIBLIOGRAPHY

Affleck, Muriel. "Recognizing the Values and Power of Play," *Early Childhood Education*, Vol. 18, #2, 1985.

Arnold, Peter. Ed. *The Book of Games*, Exeter Books, New York, 1985.

Brandeth, Gyles. *Game-a-Day Book*, Sterling, 1984.

California Department of Education. *Mathematics Framework for California Public Schools, Kindergarten Through Grade Twelve*. Sacramento, 1992.

Diagram Group. *The Way to Play*. Paddington Press, London, 1975.

Eagan, Robynne. *Game for a Game?* Teaching & Learning Company, 1995.

Elkind, David. *Child Development and Education: A Piagetian Perspective*. Oxford University Press, New York, 1976.

Ellis, Judy. *Engaging Young Learners Workshop*, Perth, Ontario, April 1995.

Fowke, Edith. Illustrated by Judith Gwyn Brown. *Ring Around the Moon*. McClelland and Stewart, Toronto, 1987.

Grunfeld, Frederic V. *Games of the World*. Published by Swiss Committee for UNICEF, Zurich, 1982.

Hayunga, Pat. "The Importance of Play in Understanding and Facilitating Early Development," *Early Childhood Education*, Vol. 18, #2, 1985.

Ministry of Education, *The Formative Years*, P1J1. Toronto, Canada, 1975.

Ministry of Tourism and Recreation, *Rec Tek's New Games Manual*, Toronto, Ontario, 1984.

Moorman, Chick dee Dishon, *Our Classroom*. Prentice Hall, Inc., Engelwood Cliffs, New Jersey.

Pentagram, compiled by. *Pentagames*. A Fireside Book/ Simon & Schuster, Inc./UNIECE, New York, 1990.

Shortz, Will. Ed. *Giant Book of Games*, Times Books/P and B Publishing Co., 1991.

Watson, Dorothy, J., ed. *Ideas and Insights, Language Arts in the Elementary School*, 1987.

Wood, Clement, and Gloria Goddard. *The Complete Book of Games*. Doubleday and Company, Inc., 1940.